Health Care Financing for Severe Developmental Disabilities

Monographs of the American Association on Mental Retardation, 14

Michael J. Begab, Series Editor

Health Care Financing for Severe Developmental Disabilities

by

Arnold Birenbaum
St. John's University New York

and

Dorothy Guyot
Herbert J. Cohen
Rose F. Kennedy Center University
Affiliated Program
Albert Einstein College of Medicine

Published by
American Association on Mental Retardation
1719 Kalorama Road, NW
Washington, DC 20009

The points of view herein are those of the authors and do not necessarily represent the official policy or opinion of the American Association on Mental Retardation. Publication does not imply endorsement by the Editor, the Association, or its individual members.

No. 14, Monographs of the American Association on Mental Retardation (ISSN 0895-8009)

Library of Congress Cataloging-in-Publication Data

Birenbaum, Arnold.
   Health care financing for severe developmental disabilities / by Arnold Birenbaum and Dorothy Guyot, Herbert J. Cohen.

   p. cm. — (Monographs of the American Association on Mental Retardation, ISSN 0895-8009)
   Includes bibliographical references.
   ISBN 0-940898-24-1 (pbk.): $22.95
   1. Mentally handicapped children—Medical care—economic aspects—United States.   2. Autistic children—Medical care—Economic aspects—United States.   3. Child health services—United States—Finance.   4. Medical policy—United States.   I. Guyot, Dorothy.   II. Cohen, Herbert Jesse, 1935-   .   III. Title.   IV. Series.
   [DNLM: 1. Autism, Infantile—economics.   2. Child health Services—economics.   3. Health Services Research—economics.   4. Mental Retardation—economics.   W1 M0559J no. 14 / WS 107 B618h]   RJ506.M4B54   1990
   338.4'33621968588'00973—dc20
   DNLM/DLC
   for Library of Congress   90-14442
                                                                                       CIP

Printed in the United States of America

Contents

Figures

Tables

Foreword

Alan Crocker
Boston Children's Hospital

The events of the 1980s have created a mandate for analysis and reform of the methods by which health care for children with disabilities is delivered and supported. These children are now securely in the community, their families have found a voice, and the medical knowledge base is considerably improved. Further, the basic values underlying the principles of care delivery have been clarified, and professional standards have been much discussed.

Dogging the system, however, are fragmented and ultimately incomplete assurances of access to services and equitable means for meeting the expense. While national costs for health care remain alarmingly high, goals are not being met for best practices in utilization of care or provision of reinforcement for families. It is clear that providers and consumers must join to obtain a better understanding of process questions and form resolves that will bring a consistent, comfortable, and productive system.

This monograph, and the project which gave rise to it, makes available critically valuable information and ideas on behalf of children, families, providers, and planners involved in services for people with developmental disabilities. In my view, this report represents an astonishing achievement. The authors have been extremely energetic in gathering a broad national sample of relevant children and families, and in employing a multimodal methodology to ensure an accurate description of service characteristics and financial information. Though the work is primarily concerned with the circumstances of childhood, the analysis continues into young adult life and speaks to the potentially difficult transition period. A huge amount of data has been combined to form strategic tables and very readable conclusions. High variability and heterogeneity within the sample has been intelligently accommodated.

The selection to study children with autism and those with severe and profound mental retardation (more than 300 of each) is commendable. These two groups provide an instructive contrast in the configuration of needed services, yet they share equally compelling effects on personal and family progress. Both are insinuated to be expensive disabilities, but their prevalence is sufficiently low that meaningful information about their issues can seldom be gleaned from the usual surveys of developmental disorders. Each is commonly included within "low incidence" tabulations, and hence accurate considerations are sparse in any one location. There are, however, about 100,000 such children and families in the nation. These individuals have deserved more careful exploration, and now they have it.

The monograph has two distinct sections. The first involves reporting and interpretation of the study data, and the second explores policy implications and makes recommendations. The first part contains a gripping story of family life in the presence of serious disability and of their search for services.It is interesting to note the variability in practice among school districts regarding acknowledgment of these diagnoses and their use as a basis for program design. A three-fold range in prevalence for autism is reported between those who devoted a special investment to this disability and those who did not.

The apparent prevalence of severe and profound mental retardation showed even greater variation (six-fold). At the time of this sample (1985-86) the authors report that all of the children with severe retardation were in special classes, and the majority were located in special schools. Mainstreaming projects had evidently not significantly affected local practices. A distribution curve is recorded for the intelligence of the children with autism; it is doubtless subject to numerous technical complications. The variation is large, with many children in the moderate range of mental retardation.

The specificity provided by this study on usage rates for medical services and on the levels of health-related costs, is extremely useful and provides an important base for the later assertions about most reasonable policy. The picture that emerges is one of real but moderate stress. The children with autism had a medical visit rate slightly above the national average, while those with severe mental retardation had 3 times the national average.

These figures were significantly influenced by the socioeconomic characteristics of the families. For autism, the hospital discharge rates were double the national average, and for children with retardation the rate was nine times the national average. The average annual health care expenditures for autism totaled $1,000; $4,000 when the child had severe mental retardation (the usual national childhood figure is $400). Few families in this report had severe degrees of annual cost (5-digit totals), and only 10% had significant cumulative medical debts.

For the children with retardation, an important qualifier was the degree of accompanying physical disability. A good ambulatory status ("the ability to walk half a mile") separated the low users of medical services from the high users. Modern interventions and technology can assuredly take the expenditures to higher levels, such as the use of computer devices for augmented communication and the procurement of motorized wheelchairs and adapted vans. However, there were few of these present in the sample. The families' out-of-pocket expenses here involved both medical care and health-related elements (such as special child care, home modifications, travel costs, and respite). These averaged $900 annually for children with autism, and $1,900 for those with severe mental retardation.

Interesting and unusual data are provided on the personal circumstances of family responsibilities in child care. Particularly arduous are the effects of the limited capability for independence which characterize these young people. In the family's judgment, less than one third of the autistic children from 10 to 24 years of age and less than one fifth of those with severe mental retardation were able to take care of themselves for even brief periods of time. Yet only a quarter of those families received regular child care from outside sources.

The goals that the authors propose as the basis for the planning of health care systems are really affirmations of fundamental values, and are well defended. They state calmly, for example, that "The birth of a developmentally disabled child should be treated as a normal risk for which insurance can provide protection." This affirmation, in my view, is inspired and logical. It removes the onus of apology or defensiveness from the negotiation, and has the quality of a human right. It can be used as the reference point during all the subsequent repair work needed to assure access and affordability.

The authors make two other statements that also deserve framing: (1) "The health care requirements of disabled and chronically ill children should be viewed broadly to include personal care and family support," and (2) "Financing should be administratively simple."

With these "goals" in place, present society can make vigorous strides toward achieving entitlement for the health care support that is appropriate for these vulnerable individuals. "Special needs" can become simply a motivation for tuning the system, rather than an origin for hand wringing.

As noted by the authors, there are substantial reforms needed in both the private and public sectors. These tend to be concentrated on reimbursement features, but there is ultimately a direct relationship to access. A key element includes state-based review of the adequacy of private insurance, including family eligibility and the configuration of benefits, with mandates to employers to achieve meaningful coverage.

We also must define the true role of reimbursement through Medicaid—is it to be for low income families only, or is it the core for the circumstances of disability? Enrollment needs simplification, and waivers need standardization. Coordination of care for families should probably be enhanced via Title V agencies (Children with Special Health Care Needs).

Finally, we have the compelling assignment of deciding if, after all, a universally applied national health insurance system is the best resolution. The climate for this bold step seems favorable. Support for families could be equitable, and the effects salutary for the conservation of human resources. The authors note that a government-financed national health plan "could prove to be the best means to meet the health care needs of children with developmental disabilities and of all Americans."

The fact that these children with autism and severe mental retardation can lead us to an understanding of the larger issues is intriguing.

_____Acknowledgments

This study was made possible through the support of the federal Division of Maternal and Child Health (HRSA/DMCH Grant #363515), the Administration for Developmental Disabilities, and the National Institute of Mental Health. From the beginning, Nathan Smith, John Powers, and Herbert Semmel were unstintingly generous in investing their energies and wisdom to make this project possible. In addition to expressing appreciation to our project officers, Aaron Favors, John Schwab, Constance McAlear, and Paul Widem, we wish to thank a far-flung team.

Members of our advisory boards gave guidance and insights without being pedantic. We thank National Advisory Board members John Butler, Judson Force, Steven A. Freedman, Willis B. Goldbeck, Henry Ireys, Donald Muse, and David Salkever. We are happy to thank the members of the Voluntary Association and Parents Advisory Board: Alan Abeson and Paul Marchand, Association for Retarded Citizens; Alan Brownstein, National Hemophilia Foundation; Robert K. Dressing, Cystic Fibrosis Foundation; Roy Morgan, Victoria Raskin and David Lorms, National Society for Children and Adults with Autism; Jackie Pitts, Spina Bifida Association; and Karen Shannon, Sick Kids Need Involved People (SKIP). We appreciate the helpful advice from members of the Medical Advisory Board, Louis Aledort, Donald Cohen, Alan Crocker, David McLone, Elaine H. Mischler, and Daniel J. Whitlock.

Across the country, educators and clinic staff introduced the study to families, for which we heartily thank them. These project coordinators are Cissi Bernhard, Penny Ray, and Carolyne Gann in Birmingham, AL; Susan Anderson, Stan Ebert, and Hope Silbert in Fresno, CA; Mary Ann Denham and Mary Ferguson in Jacksonville, FL; Ellen J. Weber, Jenny Johnson, and Julie Wood of Des Moines and Iowa City, IA; Angus McMillan, Rae Kleinbrook, James Kubaiko, Elizabeth Ampah, Mary Ann Tomasso, and Iris Berwitt for Wayne County, MI; Diane Stevens, Norma Miele, Elaina Bastick, June Goldberg, and Maria Weiner in Morris County, NJ; Arlene Schwartz, Barbara Curtis, Norma Drossman, and Deborah Cotton in Suffolk County, NY; Marilyn Monteiro and Deborah Wong in Dallas, TX. Interviewing was superbly managed by Sandra Ezrine of Survey Research Associates of Baltimore.

We particularly appreciate the careful work of staff members who joined us for months or years at various stages in the work. We thank Carol DeVictoria for applying her considerable technical and organizational skills to create coherent data sets and perform lengthy statistical analyses. Many talented individuals contributed to completing the study: Madelyn Davis, Fern Jeffries, Christine DeMuccio, JoAnne Pawlowski, Isabel Fuentes, Mary McKenna, Richard Lin, Brenda Marcano, Bridget Brown, Anusha Fernando, Timothy McCorry, Jonathan Rapollo, Steven Birenbaum, and Brigitte Naroskyin. Gerald Cohen performed a special analysis of the indirect cost of mothers foregoing employment. Colleagues at the Rose F. Kennedy Center UAP have given us advice on many technical points concerning developmentally disabled children. Here we express our thanks to Ruth Kaminer, John Powers, Rani Kathirithamby, Harold Diner, Howard Demb, Eleanora Jedrysek, Lester Zimmerman, Maris Rosenberg, and Sheryl White. We also extend special thanks to our colleagues Harriet Fox, Martin Frankel, Bob Griss, Holgar Hansen, Tormod Lunde, Margaret McManus, Paul Newacheck, Loretta O'Dell, Eva Radel, Stephen Richardson, Seymour Sudman, Victor Teglesi, Daniel Walden, Robert Wright, and Pearl Zinner for sharing their expertise.

Introduction

This monograph analyzes the utilization, expenditures, and financing of health care for children and young adults with two different types of developmental disabilities: autism and severe or profound mental retardation. The purpose of the study was to collect reliable and accurate national data useful for making public policy. Among the many policy concerns that the data address, two stand out: access to health care services and a system for equitable financing of those services.

Chapter 1 introduces the problem under study, reviews the literature, and clarifies the aims of the project:

1. To develop estimates of the patterns of health care utilization, expenditures, and financing for children, adolescents, and young adults with autism or severe or profound mental retardation.

2. To develop policy alternatives that will improve health care while containing costs.

Chapter 2 summarizes the methodology, which avoids the limitations of the standard approaches undertaken in health services research. Chapter 3 describes the children, adolescents, and young adults in the study. Chapter 4 analyzes the patterns of health care utilization, comparing the two disabilities against national averages and examining utilization rates by race, family income, and insurance coverage. It highlights the shortfalls in preventive and therapeutic care: medical check-ups, dental check-ups, and habilitative therapies.

Chapter 5 describes the variation in annual total expenditures between and within disability groups by age, family income, and other characteristics. It examines the types of direct health care expenditure using the same categories as the National Medical Care Utilization and Expenditure Survey: hospital stays, physician services during hospital stays, outpatient hospital services, physicians in private practice, dentists, services of allied health professionals, drugs, medical equipment, medical supplies. In addition, we report on a wide variety of home care expenditures necessitated by the developmental disabilities: child care, summer and weekend programs, home and car modification, replacement of items damaged by the children.

Chapters 6 through 8 analyze the patterns of financing for health care and the financial burden on the family for direct, out-of-pocket, health care expenses. In chapter 6 we look at who has private insurance, Medicaid, services from programs for Children with Special Health Needs, and other third party payers. We compare the uninsured with national averages and explore which families have been refused or limited in the insurance coverage they could obtain for their children with disabilities.

Chapter 7 examines in detail which sources paid for which types of services. We document the shift in sources of financing when the child turns 18. Chapter 8 details the financial burdens on the family of both current out-of-pocket expenditures and medical debt not only for professional services, but also for transportation, baby-sitting, meals and other incidental expenses incurred during visits to health care providers.

Chapter 9, on family hardships, examines the burdens of child care and whether they are shared. It also mentions the indirect costs of the child's disability due to the mother's foregoing paid employment in order to attend to her child's needs. With basic information on health care charges, utilization, and financing in place, we recommend policy alternatives in chapter 10. Here we assess how well different private sector and public sector strategies for reform address the needs of chronically disabled children for health insurance, for coverage of essential services, and for protection of their parents from catastrophic out-of-pocket expenses. We conclude that the major inequities found in the care of children with developmental disabilities should have high priority on the agenda for reform.

Chapter 1

The Problem and the Aims of the Study

THE PROBLEM

The Surgeon General's 1987 Report on Children with Special Health Care Needs stated that health care insurance must be made available for all children with special health care needs and their families (Public Health Service, 1987). Insurance, whether private or public, increases access to care.

There is widespread agreement that the present system of of health care financing does little to enhance the quality of life and coordination of services for children with severe chronic illnesses; nor does it create incentives to reduce costs. The comprehensive, multidisciplinary study conducted at Vanderbilt University has provided a balanced assessment of the problems of health care for children with chronic conditions and has demonstrated the need for the type of data this research has generated (Hobbs, Perrin, & Ireys, 1985).

The present patchwork system of financing has produced much discontent and some proposals, but has not led directly to new policies. One roadblock to change has been the lack of recent information on utilization, costs, and financing of health services for children with severe chronic illnesses and developmental disabilities. Without comprehensive, reliable, and systematically collected data, it is difficult for planners and analysts to develop new approaches to financing care for chronically ill and disabled children. Moreover, without expenditure and utilization data, planners cannot determine the relative impact of different financing plans. Ill-conceived insurance programs and plans are seen by medical experts as impeding the delivery of quality care. One pediatrician noted:

> The key to cost-effective high-quality health care for children is child health supervision with its preventive component. However, an inadequate understanding of the health-care needs of children and of the effects of insurance on the financing of their health care has led the health insurance industry to resist coverage of child health supervision. (Austin, 1984, p.1117)

Throughout this study we have documented examples of children not receiving appropriate preventive care.

A persistent concern among health care policy experts is the lifelong financing problems for families with seriously chronically ill and disabled members

1

(Anderson, 1985). Current policy debates on the cost of care for people with chronic illnesses, the impact of catastrophic illness insurance plans, and the appropriate roles of private and public insurance in paying for their care suggest that financing remedies for families with children with serious chronic illnesses are forthcoming.

However, accurate data and careful estimates are needed for planning and providing health care financing in support of family-centered, community-based, comprehensive care. Policymakers do not have good estimates of the cost or benefits of proposed insurance regulations and programs, and, as a result, they are reluctant to legislate new benefits programs. For children with special health care needs, this lack of baseline data on utilization, expenditures, and financing reflects the fragmentation found in the current world of health care.

THE AIMS OF THE STUDY

A grant from the federal Bureau of Maternal and Child Health and supplemental support from the Administration on Developmental Disabilities and the National Institute of Mental Health enabled the staff of the Rose F. Kennedy Center University Affiliated Program of the Albert Einstein College of Medicine to create a data base for the development of policy recommendations.

The research project studied three serious, low prevalence conditions: autism, severe and profound mental retardation, and hemophilia. This monograph reports on only the two developmental disabilities. The reason that we have included young adults up to age 24 in a study that concerns children is because among Americans as a whole health insurance coverage is least frequent among young adults. The double aim was to collect and analyze baseline data on health care utilization and expenditures for children and young adults with major developmental disabilities and to use these data in formulating policy recommendations. Autism and severe mental retardation vary on several dimensions:

- The level of physical health.
- The stability or deterioration of health.
- The degree to which the child's condition is life-threatening.
- The degree of self-reliance that the child can develop.
- The presence of physical stigmata.
- The degree of medical consensus on treatment.
- The need for intrusive and demanding routines of care.
- The degree to which generic private insurance and public programs pay for the care required by the condition.
- The extent to which special subsidy programs exist to finance extraordinary family expenses.

By studying children in these two disability categories, we aimed to answer questions that may be pertinent to a wide variety of children with low prevalence chronic conditions.

REVIEW OF THE LITERATURE

The 1977 National Medical Care Expenditures Study (NMCES) found that families are particularly burdened financially when they include people in poor health. Out-of-pocket expenses for young adults who considered themselves to be in poor health were 2.5 times higher than for those in excellent health. The families of children under six years of age who were in fair or poor health spent 1.7 times as much out-of-pocket as families of children in excellent or good health. Similar trends exist when other age brackets below 24 years of age are compared (Rossiter & Wilensky, 1982).

As reported a decade ago (National Center for Health Statistics, 1975), out-of-pocket spending for health care has taken a larger share of family income in lower income groups than in higher income groups. The fact that the lowest income groups spent proportionally more than those in higher family income brackets suggests that it is necessary to document to what extent families with children who are seriously chronically ill or developmentally disabled are particularly burdened when found in the poor or near poor income brackets.

Because the 1977 NMCES survey of 14,000 randomly selected households did not deliberately oversample individuals with disabilities or chronic conditions, it included few children with developmental disabilities and thus could not specify how income affected their access to services.

Newacheck and Halfon (1986) analyzed the 1980 National Medical Care Utilization and Expenditure Survey (NMCUES) and found that children with substantial health problems from low income families continue to lag behind their higher income counterparts (p.813) in use of ambulatory services. Moreover, less than half of these low income families with children reported to be in fair or poor health were Medicaid eligible. Within the low income group, all children with health problems that limited their usual activities who did not have Medicaid averaged 1.6 fewer physician visits than the Medicaid users and had 2.8 fewer visits annually than similarly unhealthy children from higher income families (Newacheck & Halfon, 1986).

Compared to normal children, the chronically ill are clearly heavy users of health care services. In a single site study in Cleveland that compared children with known diagnoses of serious chronic illnesses and developmental disabilities to healthy peers who were hospital clinic users from the same area, substantial differences were found in use of both ambulatory and inpatient services (Smyth-Staruch,Breslau, Weitzman, & Gortmaker, 1984). In particular, children with congenital conditions used a disproportionate amount of services from physician-specialists, occupational, speech, and physical therapists: Services used by the chronically ill and disabled children were ten times that of the comparison sample.

The ways in which public laws regulate private insurance, generate tax deduction options, and create entitlement programs under social security legislation are key elements in understanding the articulation between services and financing mechanisms for seriously disabled and chronically ill children (Hobbs et al., 1985). Typically, a seriously disabled child has a health care problem of such magnitude that federal programs, state programs, and private insurance all can be triggered into action, shaping the quality and quantity of the services delivered.

While they constitute a small proportion of the total number of children, severely disabled and chronically ill children will always require services that can help them lead a more normal life. Although only 2% of children under the age of 14 had severe limitations of activity due to health conditions, these children accounted for 12.9% of hospital discharges and almost 25% of total hospital days for that year. They also had more than three times the number of physician visits per child as children without limitations of activity (Hobbs et al., 1985).

Current Financing of Care for Seriously Chronically Ill Children with Developmental Disabilities

Since the volume of care received by seriously chronically ill and developmentally disabled children is extensive, it is reasonable to expect that the research literature on health services policy would be replete with carefully crafted studies on how services are used, how much they cost, and who paid for them. Yet some of the least understood factors contributing to poor health and quality of life—health care use, costs, and financing for chronically ill children—are hardly ever studied in depth.

In particular, no national data base exists that would permit an understanding of specific childhood illnesses and family background characteristics as these relate to amounts and sources of private and public payments, either at a single point in time or over the life of the child (Butler, Budetti, MacManus, Stenmark, & Newacheck, 1985).

The limitations and strengths of existing national data sets as they bear on children's health are carefully described by McManus, Melus, Norton, and Brauer (1986), but that is only a beginning. There is widespread agreement that a comprehensive care approach to health care for children with serious chronic illness cannot be attained within the current system of financing, oriented primarily to hospital care (Budetti, Butler, & McManus, 1982; Division of Maternal and Child Health Services, 1984; Hobbs et al., 1985).

Facing a call for action, policy analysts and planners cannot generate proposals without recently collected data that is national in scope and focused on specific disease categories. Even the much awaited report of the RAND experiment on the impact of health care coverage on utilization and health did not oversample seriously chronically ill children (Valdez et al., 1986). The RAND study, by the nature of its design, also provides no information on the impact on utilization of being uninsured. Recently Butler and his colleagues reported that health insurance coverage was a predictor of whether a disabled child had seen a doctor in the past year, even when alternative explanations such as data gathering site location, family background characteristics, type and severity of the disability, and structural access factors were controlled. Hispanic children with disabilities were more likely than white children to be without any health insurance (Butler,Singer, Palfrey, & Walker, 1987).

Any policy recommendations to assist families of seriously developmentally disabled and chronically ill children should be carefully grounded in data that demonstrate how this population differs from other families and what risks are run by not providing adequate financing. Starfield and Dutton (1985) have already raised this concern about applying the results and implications of the RAND experiment to an at-risk population.

Utilization of Services

Chronically ill children constitute a group that use an inordinately large amount of inpatient services. Butler and his colleagues reported in their 1985 study that chronic health conditions among children under age fifteen accounted for 34.8% of inpatient discharges and 36.1% of days of inpatient care in 1977 (as cited in Hobbs et al., 1985, p.172). Like their adult counterparts, children with limitations in activities were more likely to use outpatient services than their healthy peers (Newacheck & Butler, 1983).

Furthermore, it is often noted that some children with chronic illnesses use more services than others (Starfield et al., 1984). Krischer and Cook (1985) reported that, in their study of Medicaid-eligible, chronically ill children in rural Florida, "inpatient services accounted for 54.2% of the total expenditures despite the fact that 12% of the cases had been hospitalized" (p.951). Information is lacking on how to account for this variability, given the similarity of the children as far as severity of condition is concerned.

Additional data need to be collected on utilization according to access to different types of providers (e.g., specialties), practice settings (fee-for-service vs. HMOs), or comprehensive care centers. Existing studies are often limited to a single site or disease (see, for example, Meyers et al., 1972; Vance & Taylor, 1971) and do not reflect the diversity and complexity of health care delivery in the late 1980s.

While considerable literature exists that compares the efficacy and cost of home vs. hospital based service delivery (see Burr, Guyer, Todres, Abrahams, & Chiodo, 1983; Donn, 1982; Levine, 1975; Martinson et al., 1979; Moldow, Armstrong, Henry, & Martinson, 1982; Pinney & Cotton, 1976; Strawczynski, Stachewitsch, Morgenstern, & Shaw, 1973; Strayer, Kisker, & Fethke, 1980), what is lacking is a national study with a representative sample, depicting the full range of service utilization in cases of these rare but costly diseases.

One of the few national studies, based on 1,726 special education students in five large metropolitan school systems, found that substantial numbers of these pupils (26%) had no regular physician and/or had not visited a physician in the previous year (Singer, Butler, & Palfrey, 1986). However, even this excellent study was limited in scope and did not fully deal with cost, utilization, and payment burdens for families of seriously chronically ill children.

Expenditures

Little is known about the complete or total costs, both direct and indirect, for children with serious chronic illnesses. The best documentation of expenditures is for hemophilia, including comparison of home infusion to hospital administration of blood products (see Aledort & Diaz, 1982; Eyster et al., 1980; Levine, 1974, 1975; Linney & Lazerson, 1979; Meyers et al., 1972; Smith, Keyes, Forman, 1982; Strawczynski et al., 1973). Only fragmentary reports are available for other diseases and the costs of various forms of care.

McLaughlin and Shurtleff (1978) have reported on surgical and foster care expenditures for children with spina bifida, including only those children they personally treated. A Massachusetts study neglected to include non-reimbursed expenses for equipment, supplies, professional fees, and prescriptions (Callahan, Plough, & Wisensale, 1981). Ending in 1961, the long-term cost of care study for seriously chronically ill children in Erie County, New York, did collect meticulously detailed information on costs for 45 diagnostic categories (Sultz, Schlesinger, Mosher, & Feldman, 1972). Excluded, however, were diseases of current interest, such as spina bifida. Conditions such as dependence on a ventilator or other modern technology were not studied.

Detailed information on which to build national policy is extremely thin because there are few studies on the alternative costs of hospital versus home care for seriously chronically ill children. In a regional pilot project to provide home care for hospitalized ventilator-assisted patients established by the Southern California Kaiser Permanente Medical Care Program, only 4 of the 21 surviving patients were under the age of 21. Home care for these four children averaged $348 per day, compared with a daily hospital rate of $430 (Southern California Kaiser, 1987). Other detailed information on costs of care for ventilator-assisted children is based on six Massachusetts cases (Burr et al., 1983).

A study sponsored by the Bureau of Maternal and Child Health has documented costs in three home care programs for ventilator-assisted children in Illinois, Maryland, and Louisiana, but children outside these programs are outside of the study (Aday, Wegener, Anderson, & Aitken, 1989). One study of medical costs of cancer—the second most frequent childhood killer—is based on 16 cases in a shared management program in Iowa (Butler et al., 1985). As noted, policymakers wonder how to finance high cost medical technology and support services for at-risk children.

Sources of Payment

Information on insurance coverage for severely developmentally disabled and chronically ill children is based largely on scattered evidence from unpublished sources. These studies often rely on small numbers of unrepresentative cases (see McFarlane, 1982; Callahan et al., 1981; Majure, 1981; National Hemophilia Foundation, 1978; Levine, 1974; McCollum, 1971). In addition, studies that attempt to discuss more broadly the impact on the family of serious chronic illness only speculate on how restrictive insurance coverage among these families could affect the utilization of services (Meyers et al., 1972; Vance & Taylor, 1971).

Singer et al. (1986) found in a national study based on special education pupils that insurance coverage was associated with physician visits, demonstrating that 20% fewer of the uninsured than publicly or privately insured visited a physician in the previous year.

Some of the research reported in the literature reveals incomplete data collection, and there are no national studies of sources of payment for specific low prevalence diseases. The few studies that focus on out-of-pocket expenses for various diseases do not provide information on percentages and dollar amounts for reimbursed services (Lansky et al., 1979; McCollum, 1971; Strayer et al., 1980). Perrin (1986) reported that payment sources varied among procedures, indicating that some insurance policies exclude certain expensive surgeries. Self-payment varied from a low of 1.6% for tonsillectomies and adenoidectomies to 13.5% for spina bifida procedures and care. Private insurance was less likely to cover congenital heart disease surgery than the previously mentioned low technology procedures. Finally, supported by a grant from the National Institute for Handicapped Research, the Human Services Research Institute's investigation of models for financing care of chronically ill children was not based on a national sampling frame (Bradley & Agosta, 1985).

CHOICE OF TERMS

We have been careful to use terms as they have been defined in the literature of health services research. We use the terms "charges" and "expenditure" but avoid the term "cost," which means the dollar obligations that a provider had to incur in order to deliver the specific services that a specific client received. For example, should two physically healthy eight-year-olds with severe mental retardation each have a well-child visit to a pediatrician, she would charge $8 for each visit because that is the amount New York Medicaid will pay per routine visit. However, the pediatrician's cost in her time, her staff's time, and overhead might be $30 for a quick checkup with a competent mother, and the cost to serve the child of an intellectually limited mother might be $60 in time wasted for broken appointments and the pediatrician's time in slow, deliberate explanations of points that are obvious to the majority of mothers.

The term "residential placement" is comprehensive, meaning all formally established living arrangements: foster care, group homes, community residences, intermediate care facilities for mentally retarded individuals (ICF/MR), and nursing homes. In our study, the great majority of the children, adolescents, and young adults in residential placement live in foster care and other family-like settings. No connotation of a large institution should be attached to the term "residential placement."

CONCLUSIONS

As would seem evident, new research is required upon which to make policy, especially when the focus of concern is the special health care needs of people with developmental disabilities. Carefully constructed studies are needed that combine *sufficient sample size*—a feature that is not possible to find in the probabilistic approach of the national health surveys—with the *representativeness* that is missing from single site specialty clinic studies with their unrepresentative, albeit, highly convenient samples for study.

Our review of the literature indicates that there is no current and accurate basic information on the utilization, expenditures, and financing of health care services for people with developmental disabilities. Consequently, this population remains less of a concern for policymakers, who must allocate scarce health care dollars among competing interests and needs. In addition, the absence of carefully collected data on health care utilization, expenditures, and financing for developmentally disabled children, adolescents, and adults makes it impossible to conduct meaningful analyses of their special health care and related service needs. Thus, policymakers cannot attempt to address all these needs at the federal, state, and local levels of government. It is our intent to bridge these gaps in information and make a contribution to policy analysis. The next chapter describes the methods we used to conduct the study.

Chapter 2

_____Methodology

Among the wide variety of chronic illnesses and disabilities that afflict children, two low incidence conditions are the concerns of this monograph: autism, and severe and profound mental retardation. These two form a diverse set when regarded from various perspectives.

While the etiology of autism is little understood, knowledge is growing of the multiple causes of severe mental retardation. Medical opinion is divided on management of children with autism. To the casual observer, children with severe mental retardation have obvious disabilities, while higher functioning children with autism do not. Children with autism use a modest amount of health care on average, while children with severe retardation tend to have multiple physical conditions that require medical attention.

Within each disability there is great variation in the severity of the condition, in the number of comorbidities, and in functional abilities. We cannot emphasize too much the diversity within each disability category. A profound discussion of the diversity among children with mental retardation is found in the work of Stephen Richardson (1984).

We aimed to design a study that would provide estimates of costs, utilization, and financing of health care services that would be as accurate as possible, given budgetary constraints. Because one of the crucial questions is whether lack of financing impedes the access of these children to necessary health care, we provided a rough answer using the data provided by the children's primary physicians and physicians who provided specialty care for the developmental disability. A panel of pediatric specialists in developmental disability assessed the minimum number of monitoring visits each child should have received. Throughout the study we sought to provide the best possible data base upon which to base policy recommendations. Therefore, we paid close attention to questions of sampling, response rate, survey instrument design, reconciling conflicting data from different sources, and missing data.

THE SAMPLE

Our first problem was determining where we would derive a national sample for low prevalence conditions. How do researchers find subjects for a national study when their prevalence in the population is as low as 5 per 10,000? The protocol for a typical health study finds the samples in clinics, thus biasing the study toward those receiving the services offered by the clinics. We were concerned about developing a sample that represented the diversity in each disability category. If we were to avoid the bias of previous studies, we had to find agencies that cast the widest nets in the community to identify children and young adults with developmental disabilities.

Developing the Sampling Frame

We elaborated on the methodology of Butler and his co-workers (1987) in using special education school districts as sampling units in order to represent children and young adults in urban and suburban America. The federal law that requires service to children in need of special education, PL 94-142 (the Education for All Handicapped Children Act), created a decade ago the reporting system that we used as a sampling frame. Local public schools are required to keep a census of all children receiving special education, including those served by private schools. The law stipulates that the children must be offered services through the year that they turn 21. States specify their criteria within the federal guidelines for inclusion of children within specific categories. We reasoned that we could supplement this list of school age children at the upper end by reaching recent school graduates and at the lower end through early childhood programs.

The Bureau of the Census (1983) and the National Center for Education Statistics provided the frame for sampling. We developed a practical frame for multistage cluster sampling of a number of rare populations of children by using a little known census tape developed by the Bureau of the Census and the National Center for Education Statistics (Guyot & Birenbaum, 1986a). The STF 1 and STF 3 tapes aggregate by school systems all the data from the 1980 full census and sample census of population and housing. Because school districts have complete enumerations of their students, the frame closely approximates the universe.

The advantages of the frame are that: (a) it includes all states and territories; b) the demographics available on the sites include data from the 1980 census of population and housing; c) the schools can provide complete enumerations of children eligible to be in the study; and d) the children sampled in this way are more likely to represent the diversity of health care in the population than are children located through medical sites. The shortcomings of the frame are that it underrepresents children enrolled in private schools and that school administrators control the process of obtaining informed consent for participation in the study.

The Consequences of Selecting Sites in a Judgment Sample

The time and effort required to obtain permission from school administrators resulted in our decision to conduct the study in no more than a hand ful of sites. We obtained probability samples of children from seven metropolitan areas. When we combine them into a single sample, the standard tests of significance and association are not appropriate because we do not have a random sample. Following the advice of Seymour Sudman of the University of Illinois, we present our findings both as a mean for the whole sample of individuals and as a *range* of the means for individuals that were obtained at each site.

The reason for presenting means of sites is that we have a judgment sample of sites. If the research were performed anew using different sites, very likely the new overall means would be different from the ones we obtained, but it is unlikely they would fall outside the ranges we found. As we have only seven metropolitan areas, we show the range of means among them to indicate that the overall mean approximates a true rate for metropolitan areas. The range excludes the very highest and lowest sites.

By looking at the range, the reader can note whether the overall mean is near the middle of the range and can observe the width of the range. The overall means that we present are approximations, less rough when the range narrowly surrounds the overall mean. While we do not burden the reader with ranges for all tables, we have computed them, and in tables where we do not present the ranges, they are as wide as in tables where they are given. In all tables without ranges, the means were calculated without rounding and rounded off for presentation in order to emphasize that the findings are estimates.

An example of Medicaid coverage, which varies widely by state, will serve to illustrate the use of the range. Overall, the proportion of the 308 children and young adults with autism who have Medicaid coverage is 39%. However, in Jacksonville, FL, only 23% have Medicaid, while in Fresno County, CA, 62% have. These two extreme sites are excluded in the presentation of the range because it is extremely unlikely that the true national percentage is as low or as high as the percentages in these sites. The next to the lowest site is Dallas, at 26%, and the next to the highest is Detroit, at 48%. We can conclude that the true national percentage for metropolitan areas is somewhere between 26% and 48%, probably between 35% and 40%, which is where the overall mean of 39% falls.

Stratifying the Frame and Selecting the Sites

Because this frame is based on census data, many alternatives for stratification are available. To build in social and economic diversity, we chose to use the STF 3 census tape, which contains data on the income, occupation, ancestry, nativity, education, and residency of the population living in each school district. There were some practical limits to our quest for social and economic diversity. We did not have the resources to reach into rural school districts because the low prevalence of the conditions made it likely that we would find no more than 3 eligible children per 1,000 enrolled. It is not cost-effective to include rural children in a sampling frame based on school districts because of the large number of districts necessary to yield adequate numbers of eligible children.

From the listing of all 16,000 school systems in the United States, we made two types of selections to create a frame. First we identified 156 large school districts, with at least 139,000 inhabitants and about 50,000 school age children each. Second, we contacted every state special education department to identify states with special education cooperative districts, also known as intermediary districts. These are usually based on counties, serving up to 50 contiguous local school systems. The practical benefit of intermediate school districts to researchers is that a single decision process gives access to families in many small districts. Table 2.1 shows which states had special education cooperatives in 1985, when we put together our frame.

TABLE 2.1

State Administrative Arrangements for Special Education
as of August 1985

COUNTIES AS LOCAL EDUCATIONAL AGENCIES	SOME LARGE INTERMEDIARY DISTRICTS	SMALL & AD HOC INTERMEDIARY DISTRICTS	NO INTERMEDIARY DISTRICTS
Alabama	California	Arkansas	Arkansas
Florida	Connecticut	Arizona	Kentucky
Georgia	Illinois	Colorado	Maine
Hawaii	Indiana	Delaware	Massachusetts
Louisiana	Iowa	Idaho	Oklahoma
Maryland	Michigan	Kansas	Rhode Island
Nevada	New Jersey	Massachusetts	South
North Carolina	New York	Minnesota	Carolina
Utah	Pennsylvania	Missouri	Tennessee
Virginia	Montana	Nebraska	Wyoming
West Virginia		New Hampshire	
		New Mexico	
		North Dakota	
		Ohio	
		Oregon	
		South Dakota	
		Vermont	
		Texas	
		Washington	
		Wisconsin	

Note. List was compiled from information provided by the state offices for special education.

We identified 141 large special education districts and aggregated school district census data to describe each of these districts. In sum, the completed sampling frame was composed of 156 large school districts, both urban and county based, and 141 large special education cooperative districts. The frame included 53% of the U.S. population and about two-thirds of the metropolitan population.

We had data for each of the 297 primary sampling units on age composition, race, Spanish origin, foreign born, education, single parent households, work disability, type of employment, income, and poverty level. Our approach was to stratify the sample in terms of four variables that relate to health care utilization in the general population, to use our judgment in selecting one site from each strata, and then to examine the other census variables to check the degree to which the sites selected were representative. The four key variables in building the sampling frame were the percentage of families with income under $10,000, the generosity of the state Medicaid system, the percentage of the labor force in the types of industry that provide health insurance for their employees, and the number of physicians per 100,000 population.

This abstract description of the frame is made clearer by referring to the sites selected. Table 2.2 shows that Morris County, NJ, is in the upper half of the nation in terms of affluence, Medicaid generosity, private insurance coverage, and availability of physicians.

TABLE 2.2

Data Collection Sites in Terms of the Four Criteria for
Stratifying the Sampling Frame

SITE	FAMILY INCOME	GENEROUS MEDICAID	PRIVATE INSURANCE	NUMBER OF PHYSICIANS
Morris County, NJ	High	High	High	High
Wayne County, MI, excluding Detroit	H	H	H	L
Suffolk County, NY	H	H	L	–
Jefferson County, AL, excluding Birmingham	H	L	–	H
Eleven counties in central Iowa	H	L	–	L
Detroit, MI	L	H	H	–
Fresno City, CA	L	H	L	H
Fresno County, CA	L	H	L	L
Dallas, TX, and Birmingham, AL	L	L	–	H
Jacksonville, FL	Low	Low	Low	Low

Jacksonville (Duval County), FL, is in the lower half on all four variables. We have only 10 strata, rather than the full 16 that would result from every possible combination of the high-low dichotomy on each of the four variables. We combined strata that had few cases and were adjacent on employment opportunities for private health insurance or number of physicians. Note that for convenience in obtaining cooperation in the school districts in many cases we included a central city and its surrounding suburbs. In the later step of weighting the data we considered segments of each metropolitan area as a single site and combined Morris County, NJ, and Suffolk County, NY; Wayne

County and Detroit; Jefferson County and Birmingham; and Fresno city and County. We thus obtained a total of seven sites for analytic purposes.

An explanation of the variables used in constructing the sampling frame begins by noting that family income and type of industry are both from the 1980 census. Advice from Pamela Farley of the National Center of Health Services Research guided our designation of industries as high or low providers of health insurance coverage.

To create the index of Medicaid generosity, we extended the work of Davidson (1979; Davidson, Friedman, & Mannheim, 1985) by using five subscales. First, states were ranked from one to four according to breadth of coverage of the population, i.e., what proportion of the poor and near poor were eligible for medical assistance. Income eligibility for medical indigence in California was found at a monthly income of $801 for a family of four, but eligibility in Texas ended at $295.

Second, because the study deals with serious chronic illness and disability, we used another four-position ranking of states according to depth of services covered. Specifically, we gave one point for each of these services: rehabilitative services, occupational, physical, and speech therapy (Health Care Financing Administration, 1987).

Third, limits on hospital inpatient days varied from states with no upper limit to those with as few as 20 days per year. Again a four-position ranking scheme was created.

Fourth, the states varied in the extent to which they provided both a child spend-down provision for families with exceptional medical expenditures and a medically needy family provision for families of limited means. We reasoned that states providing both options were more generous than states that established only one, and that the child spend-down provision was more appropriate for the population under study than the medically needy provision. The absence of both constituted the lowest possible score in this four-part scale.

Fifth, beyond the state medical assistance programs themselves, one other provision was added; the percentage of the state's revenues spent on programs for the economically needy. Again, states were ranked from 1 to 4 on this variable. Scored 1 for most generous and 4 for least generous on the 5 subindexes, states were ranked on a scale of generosity, with 5 representing the greatest and 20 the least generous possibilities.

States actually scored between 5 and 17, with the best-served half of the nation's population in states scoring between 5 and 11. Table 2.3 shows the states according to level of generosity. Note that generally the Southern states are in the bottom third and the industrialized states in the top third.

Data on physicians in civilian practice came from the Bureau of the Census' *State and Metropolitan Area Data Book*, 1983 and the *County and City Data Book*, 1983. At the last stages of picking one site from each stratum, we used criteria developed by Henry Ireys to select sites from states that have diverse services in their programs for Children with Special Health Needs (Ireys & Eichler, 1988).

TABLE 2.3

Generosity of State Medicaid Programs

LEAST GENEROUS	GENEROUS	MOST GENEROUS
Alabama	Colorado	California
Alaska	Delaware	Connecticut
Arizona	Hawaii	Illinois
Arkansas	Indiana	Maine
Florida	Iowa	Massachusetts
Georgia	Kansas	Michigan
Idaho	Kentucky	Minnesota
Louisiana	Maryland	New Jersey
Mississippi	Missouri	New York
Nevada	Montana	Pennsylvania
New Mexico	Nebraska	Rhode Island
South Carolina	New Hampshire	Vermont
South Dakota	North Carolina	Wisconsin
Tennessee	North Dakota	
Texas	Ohio	
Virginia	Oklahoma	
West Virginia	Oregon	
Wyoming	Utah	
	Washington	

Note. Five criteria were used to create this 1985 ranking: proportion of low-income people eligible, coverage of therapeutic services, coverage of hospital stays, inclusions of non-poor families with high medical expenses, and state provision of services for the needy.

The Sites in the Study

The seven metropolitan areas where the children were served by a total of 13 school districts were selected in a judgment sample to reflect some of the diversity of the American health care system. The Northeast and the largest metropolitan areas are represented by Suffolk County, NY, and Morris County, NJ. For analytic purposes these two counties within the New York City metropolitan area were treated as a single site. The North Central census region, the Midwest, is represented by Detroit and suburban Wayne County, MI, and by 11 counties in central Iowa.

The South is represented by Jacksonville, FL, Birmingham and suburban Jefferson County, AL, and Dallas, TX. The West is represented by Fresno County, CA. Table 2.4 provides some basic demographics drawn from the 1980 census. Black children were deliberately oversampled, at 27% of the sample, in order to give a higher probability of statistical significance to comparisons of white and minority group children.

Drawing the Sample at the Sites

Most school districts served sufficient numbers of severely retarded children and young adults to require sampling, but because children with autism are so rare, we drew a 100% sample in three-quarters of the sites. In sites where we sampled less than 100%, we determined the total number of respondents desired to make the sample more representative in terms of central city and suburban residents and by geographic region. Then we drew random samples of the eligible children and young adults by stratifying into 5-year age groups and selecting equal numbers from each stratum. In some sites where the school systems did not know of children under age 5, we went to clinics to include samples of younger children.

TABLE 2.4

1980 Demographics of the Sites

SITE	POPULATION AGES 0-24 (in '000s)	% FAMILIES IN LOWEST 5TH IN INCOME	% FAMILIES IN HIGHEST 5TH IN INCOME	MDs PER 100,000 POPULATION	PERCENT BLACK	PERCENT SPANISH
Northeast						
Suffolk County, NY	551	12%	34%	151	6%	5%
Morris County, NJ	161	7	48	184	3	3
Midwest						
Detroit, MI, area	987	21	32	160	36	2
Des Moines, IA, area	250	16	20	115	3	1
South						
Jacksonville, FL	242	25	24	170	25	2
Birmingham, AL, area	227	25	20	267	35	1
Dallas school district	340	22	23	213	31	13
West						
Fresno County, CA	225	23	22	170	5	29
Average for sites	436	19.5	27.8	182	22	6
United States	93,033	20%	20%	174	12%	6%

Note. Data are from *County and City Data Book, 1983,* by the Bureau of the Census, 1983, Washington, DC: U.S. Government Printing Office.

Weighting the Sample

If the data were used without weighting, we would have three sources of bias. First, the primary sampling units overrepresent cities. Second, we chose sites that have a large proportion of black residents because we wanted to have a sufficiently large sample to obtain statistical significance. And third, the coverage of the sample was extremely uneven among sites.

We consulted with Seymour Sudman of the University of Illinois and followed his advice to develop and implement an appropriate weighting scheme. The most important decision was to weight the sample to represent cities and suburbs only. Despite efforts to find large school districts outside cities and suburbs, we were able to select only an 11 county area in Iowa, centered on Des Moines, and one large agricultural county, Fresno, CA. We agreed with Sudman's assessment that these two sites were insufficient to represent rural America and decided to weight the sample to represent residents of central cities and suburbs.

From the Census Bureau we obtained available estimates for 1986 and, as necessary, extrapolated from 1980 to make estimates of the size of the 1986 civilian population from birth through 24 years of age in metropolitan areas within each of the nine census regions, broken down by ethnicity into non-Hispanic white, non-Hispanic black, and Hispanic and other. This procedure created 27 cells.

We then compared the proportion of our autism and mental retardation samples in each of these cells with the national proportion. We worked on the widely accepted assumption that both autism and severe and profound mental retardation are evenly distributed throughout the population. We assigned a weight to each individual in our study to make the proportion of the sample in each cell equal to the proportion of the metropolitan population ages 0-24 in that cell.

The results of this weighting scheme for the autism sample were that 69 out of the 308 cases received weights of less than .33 while 32 received weights greater than 3.0, the highest being 4.2. In the mental retardation sample, 75 of 326 cases received weights less than .33 and 4 cases received weights greater than 3.0, the highest being 3.5. The most substantial downward weighting occurred in Detroit and the large upward weighting was scattered among Jacksonville, Birmingham, and Fresno.

The inclusion of children living at home as well as those who were in residential placement is one of the strengths of this study because it permits direct comparison of health care utilization and expenditures. However, we have no national or local data that show what proportion of severely developmentally disabled children are in residential placement, and warn the reader not to use our data to estimate the proportion of children in placement.

We have three reasons for believing that the proportions we found are not accurate. First, for some sites we do not know whether or not there was a differential in declining to participate, but we suspect that problems of obtaining consent from institutions made the decline rate higher for children in residential placement. Second, our sampling procedure prevented us from locating any children in placement in Suffolk County. Finally, we found extreme variation among sites in use of placement. Selection of a few different sites could produce a much higher or much lower total proportion in residential placement. When we weighted the data we did not take residential placement into account and are pleased to report that the placement proportions in each disability group and among children and young adults remained substantially the same.

Before weighting, the proportions for autism were 95% at home among children and 81% among young adults. Afterward, the proportions were 92% and 80%. For children with mental retardation, the proportion before weighting was 83% at homes which changed to 86% after weighting; for young adults, the proportion changed from 64% to 62%.

Working with School Districts to Reach Eligible Families

As of 1984, 4.3 million children of the public school population of 40 million received special education services on the basis of nine categories of disability established by the federal Department of Education. The disabilities in descending order of size are learning disabled, speech impaired, mentally retarded, emotionally disturbed, hearing impaired, multiply handicapped, orthopedically impaired, visually handicapped, and deaf-blind (Office of Special Education and Rehabilitative Services, Clearing House on the Handicapped, 1985).

Within the federal guidelines, states specify their inclusion of children within additional categories. For mental retardation, the criteria are fairly standard among states. Children are classified as trainable mentally handicapped if their IQ scores are below 25, as educable mentally handicapped if their scores are between 26 and 50, and as severely multiply impaired if they are both retarded and physically disabled. However, the fact that autism is not one of the federal categories makes for inconsistencies in identifying autistic children, which contributed to the disparity in prevalence rates found across sites in our sample.

Unlike the age limits of 5 to 18 for the typical school population, 21 is the upper limit for young adults with the most severe mental disabilities because Public Law 94-142 requires they be served through the year of their 21st birthday. In addition, case finding of very young disabled children in 1984 was systematic in seven states and partial in about a dozen others. With national implementation of the early intervention program, P.L. 99-457, disabled infants will be identified from birth.

For researchers, using either medical centers or schools for the sampling frame presents a logistical problem, as only personnel of these agencies are privy to the lists of children, and, consequently, they must be the intermediaries who obtain informed consent for participation (Kearney, Hopkins, Mauss, & Weistiet, 1983). A system of local project coordinators was used in a study conducted by the Boston Children's Hospital (Butler et al., 1985). We followed this approach to obtain formal consent for cooperation from the school district and then engaged a respected member of the school district as the project coordinator, who contacted the family to obtain consent. Project coordinators have obtained information on basic demographic characteristics of the refusers and participants, which permits some generalizations about the refusers.

Efforts to obtain the highest possible participation by families began with site selection. Efforts were made to find out as much as possible about eligible districts by conversing with third parties who had administrative contact with the leadership of the eligible local educational agencies. In all states where potential sites were located, state directors of special education were called in order to find out whether or not the local educational agency kept good records and had a computerized data base, the local director of special education was considered to be a cooperative person, and any researchers had experienced problems in working in that particular district. At the same time, when we were encouraged by the state director's report, we asked for support in gaining the assistance of the local educational agency for study participation.

We then called the directors of pupil personnel services or special education at the proposed sites and asked many questions about recordkeeping and the organization of services in the district for children with autism or severe mental retardation. We explained that we wanted to work closely with an employee of the local educational agency who could be designated as the project coordinator for this field effort. The creation of this position was necessary to protect the privacy of families, who remained unknown to the research team until they agreed through an informed consent process to be in the study.

The consent form that parents signed permitted the researchers both to conduct the interview and to obtain records on the child's medical visits from providers and payers. Unfortunately, the legal language necessary to authorize the release of private records is upsetting to some parents and reduced the proportion consenting to be interviewed.

Face-to-face meetings were held at all prospective data collection sites with the director of special education, the data processing personnel who would generate lists of children according to disability, program directors responsible for pupil education, and, when possible, the person recommended for the position of project coordinator.

To promote effectiveness, project coordinators were convened in New York for an orientation and training session before they approached the families. Ultimately, however, we were dependent on their efforts to bring families into the study. The weakness of this approach is that school personnel who are inexperienced in survey research are the sole contact with the families; its strength is that school personnel know personally the families invited to participate in the survey.

In our work with the school districts, we found that the personal commitment and skill of the project coordinator was directly responsible for the proportion of the sample covered. Table 2.5 shows the number of individuals in the sample in each area and the percentage who participated in the survey.

TABLE 2.5

The Sample Initially Drawn and Percentage Participating in the Study

SITE	AUTISM		SEVERE MENTAL RETARDATION	
Northeast				
Suffolk County, NY	101	48%	50	58%
Morris County, NJ	21	67%	42	52%
Midwest				
Detroit area	203	60%	124	48%
Des Moines area	47	60%	121	63%
South				
Jacksonville	18	50%	66	29%
Birmingham area	38	55%	110	56%
Dallas	100	47%	50	18%
West				
Fresno area	35	60%	97	51%
Total	563	55%	660	49%

Almost all of the attrition in the sample was due to parents initially declining to sign the consent form. The survey firm, Survey Research Associates of Baltimore, achieved an outstanding completion rate of 97% for those with working telephone numbers.

THE SURVEY INSTRUMENTS

The survey instrument used in the telephone interviews with the family was adapted from the work of the National Center for Health Statistics (NCHS) for the 1980 National Medical Care Utilization and Expenditure Survey (NMCUES) and from the National Center for Health Services Research for the 1987 National Medical Expenditure Survey (NMES). In order to explore causes of variation in utilization and expenditures, we constructed structural equation models to identify concepts for which variables should be created (Guyot & Birenbaum, 1986b). The questionnaire covered these topics:

Household composition, employment, and income

Functional ability of the child

Child care and program participation

Financing of health care and case management

Genetic counseling

Medication for autism

Usual sources of health care

Health care providers: hospital, short term residential stays, dental, emergency room, outpatient departments, physicians in private practice, allied health professionals

Equipment, drugs, and supplies

Barriers to care, psychological counseling for the family

Residential placement

Data Collection

The families in the survey each participated in a telephone interview that covered medical visits for the three preceding months. The questionnaire inquired about each type of health care and each type of payer in the same order as the NMES and with the same wording. Based on the early experience of the National Center for Health Services Research (1980) and subsequent work on NMCUES, prior to the telephone calls, we mailed a calendar with a pocket to the families for recording their child's visits and keeping their medical bills.

We also followed NMCUES and NMES procedures by using a three-month reference period for ambulatory visits, but we asked for a year's experience of hospitalizations because an NCHS study showed quite accurate recall for hospital stays. In designing the survey to fit budget constraints, we interviewed each family only once, unlike the national studies, which interviewed the families every three months for a year.

In our telephone interview we asked the families for the names, addresses, and phone numbers of all health care providers who had served their child within the previous 12 months (July 1985—June 1986), whom we contacted in the second phase of data collection. If the child or young adult were in residential placement, both the mother and the primary caretaker replied to appropriate questions.

In developing several subsections of the questionnaire, we drew upon the standard questions used by the Census Bureau and the Bureau of Labor Statistics and also drew upon collegial advice. In consultation with Judson Force, M.D., the Director of the Maryland Children with Special Health Care Needs Program, we developed a functional disability scale that we applied to all respondents over the age of four in order to make comparisons across disability categories.

In consultation with Howard Demb, M.D, of the Rose F. Kennedy Center, we developed questions on use of medication in the treatment of autism. We developed questions on genetic counseling in consultation with Vincent Riccardi, M.D., Medical Director of the ALFIGEN-Genetics Institute of Pasadena, and with Harold Nitowsky, M.D., and Gay Sachs of the Rose F. Kennedy Center.

To obtain 12 months' records of medical visits and the primary physicians' judgments on their patients' disabilities, we contacted care providers by adapting to our circumstances the methods of the National Center for Health Statistics pilot study of cost of cancer care (Survey Research Laboratory, 1982). In attempting to collect data from many different sources about the same medical events, we created new problems: how to track our efforts to contact providers and payers from the information given to us by parents and how to derive useful information from the forms sent to us by these organizations.

A relational database designed by Victor Teglasi enabled us to keep track of mailings to over 2,000 providers and payers, but we were not able to interpret the information from these sources in such an automated fashion. Generally our staff had to decipher the forms from providers and payers, and they frequently had to call the various billing departments of hospitals for clarification on what was paid and by which payer.

RESOLVING CONFLICTING DATA

Our aim was to obtain data that were as accurate as possible on the type and volume of services each child used, the expenditure for each type of health care service, and the amount each source paid for each type of service. However, we had to resolve inconsistencies among data coming from different sources. Multiple sources of data multiply the time and effort that must be invested in data cleaning. For each of the 634 children and young adults in the study, we usually had data from three or more sources describing health care visits. The basic source was the family questionnaire, which provided a 12-month screener and visit level data for three months. The providers from whom we received data on 12 months of services were: hospital inpatient records, hospital outpatient departments and emergency rooms, physicians in private practice including attendings during hospital stays, and residential institutions ranging from ICF/MRs to foster agencies.

We also noted the child's primary physician and physician who provided disability care to provide an etiological and diagnostic assessment for an appraisal of whether or not the child would benefit from speech therapy or physical therapy and, for autism, what medications, if any, were prescribed for behavior control. From residential institutions we obtained data on the type of institution and the charges, using a form which we developed in consultation with K. Charlie Lakin of the University of Minnesota.

Accuracy in estimating emergency room usage proved more difficult than for other types of visits. After identifying from parents' reports all emergency rooms visited during the year and the child's specific visits during the three-month reference period, we were able to obtain full billing records from less than one third of the emergency rooms. Additional data obtained from outpatient billing were occasionally ambiguous as to whether the visit was to the emergency room (ER) or to a clinic; the data from Medicaid was often ambiguous; and the data from private insurance was usually ambiguous.

Our estimates of ER use are conservative in that we counted ambiguous visits as clinic visits. Further, the national tables from NMCUES include emergency room visits that result in hospitalization, accounting for 14% of all emergency room visits (National Center for Health Statistics, 1987). We excluded this usage because we could not distinguish the route of hospital admission.

We focused initially on the three-month reference period, using provider and payer data to correct information from the families. The payers from whom we received 12 months of data were: Children with Special Health Care Needs Programs (CSHN), private insurers, Health Maintenance Organizations (HMOs), and Medicaid. In handling data on the nine months beyond those the family reported, we first examined instances where two sources were inconsistent on the number of visits. We re-examined the raw data and made necessary corrections. For instance, if we received a record of three visits from a hospital clinic but a record of two visits from insurance, we recorded three visits, of which two were reimbursed by insurance.

TABLE 2.6

Parents' Knowledge of Health Care Charges

PARENTS' KNOWLEDGE	HOSPITAL STAYS N=194	PHYSICIANS IN PRIVATE PRACTICE N=595	OUTPATIENT CLINICS N=337	EMERGENCY ROOMS N=88	DENTISTS N=177
Knew exactly	36.6%	44.0%	27.6%	19.3%	35.6%
Estimated	12.4	3.9	5.6	9.1	15.8
Did not know	50.9	52.0	66.9	71.5	48.6
Total	100	100	100	100	100
Source of payment for visits where the parents *did not know* the charge					
Family or insurance	2.0	4.2	13.1	15.9	8.5
Medicaid	34.5	37.5	37.7	46.6	36.7
Children with Special Health Needs Program	7.7	0.8	3.9	1.1	1.7
Health Maintenance Organization	3.6	4.5	1.5	3.4	0.6
Free from provider	3.1	5.0	10.7	4.5	1.1

Note. The percentages shown for the sources of payment equal the percent of parents who did not know.

Similarly, where we found extra visits (above the amount reported by a provider) from a source such as an HMO or CSHN, a new variable was created, indicating the number of visits added. This could then be added to the provider amount to give a new total. These newly created variables served as flags that we used later when imputing charges.

Table 2.6 provides detail on the expenditure data that the families provided. Note that parents could report the exact charge for about one-third of the hospital stays, somewhat more for visits to physicians' offices, and somewhat less to hospital clinics. The bottom half of the table shows which source paid the bill where the family could not even estimate the charge. Overall, parents had no knowledge of charges for half the visits, and Medicaid was the predominant payer of charges unknown to the parents. If we had not invested enormous effort to obtain data from providers and payers, our knowledge of expenditures would have been rudimentary.

HANDLING MISSING DATA THROUGH IMPUTATION

We decided to use imputation for missing visit data rather than to perform analyses with data missing. Because the missing data are scattered across cases, omitting all cases with any data missing would substantially reduce the sample size and bias the sample. Omitting in any particular analysis the cases with data missing on the relevant variables would still bias the sample. The most important consideration was that there were more cases of missing data for uninsured and privately insured children than among children on Medicaid. Dropping cases with missing values would have severely biased the sample toward Medicaid recipients.

After conferring with Graham Kalton of the University of Michigan Institute for Social Research, we adapted to our needs a form of hot deck imputation called flexible matching imputation (Kalton, 1983). To initiate imputations, we first divided health care services into six categories: hospital inpatient; outpatient clinics; emergency rooms; physicians in private practice; dentistry; and therapists of all types. Because we found a moderate association in levels of usage among physicians, outpatient clinics, and emergency rooms, we performed the imputation simultaneously for these three services.

Our first round of imputations was within cases, and our second was across cases. We performed an imputation within a case where there was information from a fraction of the providers, as from two or three out of four physicians. If there was information from only one of four physicians we did nothing, leaving the value for a later imputation across cases. We developed rules to estimate the number of visits for a child when we heard from some but not all of the providers. Having found a higher response rate from physicians who are the child's usual source of care, we estimated that the returns were disproportionately from physicians who had treated the child more than the average number of times.

The procedure we followed for within-case imputation is illustrated here. Suppose the child has three physicians and two of them replied telling us of six visits. The minimum number of visits is six plus one more from the physician who failed to report, or seven. The likely maximum we selected was nine, on the assumption that the unknown physician provided an average number of visits. We then gave a weighting of 1 to the likelihood that there were nine visits, a weighting of 2 to the likelihood of eight visits and a weighting of 3 to the likelihood of seven visits. Thus, in using a table of random numbers, we were likely three times out of six times (3 + 2 + 1) to draw the number seven as the number of visits.

In other words, we used an algorithm that computed the minimum number of visits that the child could have to physicians and the likely maximum as a straight extrapolation of the number of known visits divided by the percentage of the providers covered. We gave the highest probability to the minimum number of visits and let the probability decline one step for each visit beyond the minimum.

If the child had insurance and the number of visits reported by insurance was above the minimum number, the insurance claim was taken as the total. If the child's insurance claims were below the total, we assumed that the family did not submit insurance claims for those visits.

We used a technique of flexible matching to impute across cases. At the start of this imputation, we had more than 400 cases with full 12-month visit data on visits to physicians, outpatient departments, and emergency rooms. Data for the 12-month period were missing for 21% of cases regarding visits to private physicians, 10% regarding outpatient clinics, and 10% regarding dental visits. When extra visits were added through imputation, we flagged them for a later imputation of charges. For example, suppose a child had received services from two physicians and one reported 4 visits, but the other did not reply. Suppose further that the imputation procedure resulted in assigning 2 visits to the second physician. It was necessary to know that the existing record of charges from physicians covered only the 4 reported visits and not the new total of 6 visits. The flag on the 2 imputed visits identified them as requiring an imputation of charges.

The process of imputation of data from cases with visit information to cases lacking visit information also followed a systematic procedure. To identify the variables that best predict the use of health care, we ran regressions separately on the two disability categories and whether the children had public or private insurance. The theoretical basis for the regressions was a set of structural equation models that we developed and refined. We divided the cases among cells according to this hierarchy:

Disability;

Residential placement or at home;

Number of hospital admissions 0, 1, 2 and up;

Family income in thirds.

A random procedure selected the matched case for the child. If there were a complement between the types of visit information missing, the cases swapped data. For instance, if child A had an unknown number of Outpatient Department (OPD) visits, we found the set of children who had a known number of OPD visits and matched on disability, living at home or away, number of hospital admissions, and family income. We randomly selected child B from that set, and child A received the missing data from child B. If there were no child who matched on family income, we went to the next level of the hierarchy until we could make a match. We never made matches outside of the disability category.

ESTABLISHING THE APPROPRIATE LEVEL OF PHYSICIAN MONITORING SERVICES

Across each disability in the study, we found a highly skewed distribution of use of each type of health care. Most children received modest amounts of health care and a few received a great deal of specialist care.

To estimate the number of physician visits that a child would require during a 12-month period to monitor his or her condition, we constituted a small panel of pediatricians specializing in developmental disabilities, Ruth Kaminer, M.D., Lester Zimmerman, M.D., and Howard Demb, M.D. They made independent judgments of the minimum number of ambulatory physician visits the child should have based on reports from the parents and from the primary physician or the disability physician concerning etiology and chronic conditions.

These judgments are the basis for the analyses presented in Table 4.7 and discussed on the following pages concerning the likelihood that children with social disadvantages will have as many visits as children with social advantages. As appropriate, we used either ordinary least squares or two stage regression to identify causal variables significant at .05 before computing the odds ratio.

Criteria for Physician Visit Frequency

The following criteria are arranged in a list of conditions present in the children in the sample. Our medical panel developed these criteria to judge how many ambulatory physician visits during a year a child should have for autism and for severe mental retardation and associated physical disabilities for health maintenance and for acute care visits due to hospitalization. For each condition present, the specified number of visits are added to reach an annual total for each child. The criteria are based on the existing care standards of the Children's Evaluation and Rehabilitation Center of Albert Einstein College of Medicine, one of the leading centers for developmental disability.

Checkup. The child should receive health maintenance visits according to the American Academy of Pediatrics (AAP) standard (AAP, 1977).

AGE	ANNUAL VISITS
<1	5.0
≥1 and <2	2.0
≥2 and <5	0.5
≥5 and <10	0.3
≥11 and <15	0.5
≥15 and <21	0.2

Severe and Profound Mental Retardation and Autism. The recommended number of visits annually to monitor mental development will normally be made to the pediatrician who does the health maintenance examination, which also serves the purpose of monitoring mental development. Hence, the AAP standard for visits scheduled for birth to age 2 is sufficient. Additional visits start after age 2.

AGE	ANNUAL VISITS
<2	no additional visits
≥2 and <3	2.0
≥3	0.5

Diagnosis. The child whose diagnosis of developmental disability has been completed within the reference year will have had one physician visit to report the diagnosis. We are conservatively assuming additional visits at two-month intervals to make the diagnosis.

Psychological Assessment for a Child with Autism. If the child has autism and has an IQ above 70, he or she should have 2 visits to a psychiatrist for assessment regarding behavioral problems before age 24.

Difficulty in Ambulation. For a child who can neither climb 10 stairs nor walk half a mile without assistance, additional visits are recommended for monitoring by the pediatrician or an orthopedist in addition to the monitoring already planned for the well child and for the child with severe retardation. If the child either climbs or walks, but not both, monitoring visits are half the following.

AGE	ANNUAL VISITS
≥1 and <6	2.0
≥6	1.0

Visits to an Orthopedist for Problems of Ambulation. With the growth of the child who can neither walk nor climb, the need may arise for services of an orthopedist. With the assumption that corrective surgery would take place before the age of 6, this is the recommended schedule of visits to an orthopedist.

AGE	ANNUAL VISITS
<1	1.0
≥1 and <6	2.0
≥6 and <13	1.0
≥13 and <18	0.5
≥18	0.3

Scoliosis. If the child with scoliosis can climb and walk, visits to monitor the scoliosis should be one per year. If the child has difficulty walking, monitoring for scoliosis are included in the category "Difficulty in Ambulation," except for adolescents, who need additional visits.

AGE	ANNUAL VISITS
>13 and <18	1.0

Duchenne's Muscular Dystrophy. The child will require monitoring visits at an increasing frequency because of the progressive nature of the disease. The rate of additional visits is 1 per year if the child is 12 or under and 2 per year if the child is over 12.

Orthopedic Equipment. If the child at any age receives appliances during the reference year, then for each item these additional visits should be made. For multiple items these additional visits are added, except for shoes and braces.

Braces	3.0
Wheelchair	2.0
Corrective shoes without braces	2.0
Other devices (e.g., splints)	1.0

Seizures. The pediatrician will manage the seizures of those whose management is easy and refer the difficult ones to a neurologist. If the physician notes seizures as a problem, following is the rate of additional monitoring. A good deal of monitoring of the medication can take place over the phone. This variable also includes monitoring of autistic children on medication to modify their behavior. (Details provided by some parents on the frequency of seizure were taken into account to increase the recommended number of visits.)

AGE	ANNUAL VISITS
<6	2.0
≥6 and <13	1.0
≥13 and <16	2.0 (in autism)
≥16	1.0 (in severe mental retardation)

Vision. For vision problems (but not for blindness) the child should see an ophthalmologist on this schedule. If the child gets new glasses during the year, add 1 visit.

AGE	ANNUAL VISITS
<6	2.0
≥6	1.0

Chronic Otitis. At any age there should be 2 additional visits.

Myringotomy Tubes. Add 2 visits per year.

Parkinson's Disease. Add one visit per year for monitoring at any age.

Hydrocephalus. An extra visit is required in the first year of life. The monitoring that older children require is taken into account in the monitoring for associated conditions.

Myelomeningocele. We assume that surgical correction is completed. Monitoring visits to a urologist are appropriate and are needed with increased frequency in adolescence.

AGE	ANNUAL VISITS
>1 and <3	1.0
≥3 and <13	0.5
≥13	1.0

Cardiac Problems. Because a heart condition is usually corrected early, we assume that it has been corrected in all the children. Additional checkups with a cardiologist or a pediatrician should follow this schedule.

AGE	ANNUAL VISITS
<6	2.0
≥6 and <10	1.0
≥10	0.5

Respiratory problems. If the child has difficulty breathing or chronic asthma, as noted by the parents, or a chronic respiratory condition, usually as noted by the physician, then the following additional visits are appropriate.

AGE	ANNUAL VISITS
<12	2.0
≥12	1.0

Cancer. If the child has a neoplasm, the number of ambulatory visits could be very high to monitor chemotherapy or in connection with surgery. A conservative estimate, in the absence of knowledge of the site of the neoplasm and its state, is to assume 2 monitoring visits per year at any age.

Hospital Stay. The child should have at least one ambulatory visit after hospital discharge. A good procedure for admissions is that the child see the physician who then makes the decision to admit, rather than the child going to the emergency room for admission. For all ages we assume an appropriate minimum is 2 ambulatory visits per hospital stay.

Other Conditions. For children with the following conditions that frequently accompany or form the etiology of severe and profound mental retardation, no additional visits are judged to be required: cleft palate; phenylketonuria; mucopolyssacharidosis; cytomegalovirus infection; allergies (including bronchial or atopic asthma), fishers', sickle cell, tuberous sclerosis.

Monitoring sometimes is additional for the following problems depending upon the child's other conditions: gastrointestinal problems, genitourinary infections, other chronic infections, endocrine problems, problems in the lymphatic system, and circulatory system problems.

Here we end the discussion of specific methods. Throughout the project we sought to create a valid and reliable data base. The geographic and socioeconomic diversity of the sites and the use of probability to select the sample from each site increase the likelihood that the sample as a whole is representative of American cities and suburbs. The use of many data sources to describe a year's health care events gives some assurance that the estimates are accurate. The next chapter provides details on the characteristics of the individuals in the study.

Chapter 3

A study that seeks to describe accurately the utilization, expenditures, and financing of health care for seriously developmentally disabled individuals must be sure that it reaches the target population. Even within the categories of autism and severe and profound mental retardation, there are still behavioral variability and differences in the extent to which comorbidities exist. In this chapter we explain how we arrived at the criteria for determining eligibility for inclusion in the sample. First we will define and describe autism, a developmental disorder upon which experts hold a variety of opinions.

CHARACTERISTICS OF THE SAMPLE

Autism

A commentary on autism is provided by DeMeyer, Hingtgen, and Jackson (1981).

> Infantile autism is a type of developmental disorder accompanied by severe and, to a large extent, permanent intellectual and behavioral deficits. (p.92)

A description of the usual symptoms of autism is provided by Allen (1988).

> It is well recognized that children with 'autistic features' constitute a very heterogeneous population. There is a growing consensus that the core symptoms seen in autism include deficits in: (1) social/affective/behavioral functions, (2) developmental language disorders with concomitant deficits in interpersonal communication, and (3) play/preferred activities/preoccupations which have a repetitive or stereotypic quality. (p.549)

The sample of persons with autism included 251 children and 57 young adults. The initial diagnoses were made in 65% of the cases when the children were under the age of five. In order to guard against sampling children who would not be appropriate for the study, we collected data from pupil records concerning the criteria by which the children were assigned to special education programs.

Of the entire sample of 308, in 112 cases we obtained no information on how the school reached a diagnosis of autism. Were medical diagnoses made prior to placement in special classes for children with autism? We were able to obtain information to answer this question in the records of only 180 sample members (See table 3.1). In the majority of these cases, no medical diagnosis was used in the educational placement decision. DSM III diagnoses were ascertained in only 75 cases.

TABLE 3.1

DSM-III Diagnoses for Children and Young Adults
with Autism (N = 180)

DIAGNOSIS	%
No Medical diagnosis used in the educational placement decision	58
Infantile autism–full syndrome present	19
Infantile autism–residual state	8
Childhood onset–full syndrome present	12
Childhood onset–residual state	<1
Atypical developmental disability	2

The absence of medical diagnoses prior to placement does not indicate a lack of sophistication in evaluating children suspected of being autistic, nor does it suggest mistakes in this process. Placement of children in special classes is not always dependent on medical diagnoses. We can only infer that a psychological assessment was made according to the regulations governing placement in special education classes.

While the distinction between autism and autistic tendencies within a single school system probably reflects the severity of the child's behavioral problems, valid comparisons cannot be made among districts. For instance, Dallas classified 90% in this category as "autistic," while Jacksonville and Suffolk County classified all of the children they serve as "autistic-like."

Parents describe their autistic children as physically active, unable to communicate, unable to socialize, and often unable to perform essential activities of daily living. The behaviors often exhibited by children with autism include difficulty in mixing with other children, a stand-offish manner, impaired language ability, inappropriate attachment to objects, sustained interest in objects that have repetitive motion, resistance to change in routine, and uneven development of gross and fine motor skills.

A number of different standardized autism tests could have been used by the school evaluation teams, but they were infrequently employed in determining class placement. Only 59 children were tested with instruments for autism. The most frequently used test, the Childhood Autism Rating Scale, was used in only 23% of the 59 cases, mainly in Dallas. A second test used was the Psycho-Education Profile. The remaining cases were diagnosed without standardized autism tests.

IQ results were obtained for 84% of the autistic children and young adults. Figure 3.1 displays the distribution of IQ scores for the sample, showing few in the normal range of intelligence. Fifty percent have IQ scores below 50, and over 75% have scores below 70, based on Stanford Binet and WISC tests. This distribution is roughly similar to the one found in the Nova Scotia epidemiological survey (Bryson, Clark, & Smith, 1987). Educational programs were held predominantly in special schools (64%) or in special classes in regular schools (32%).

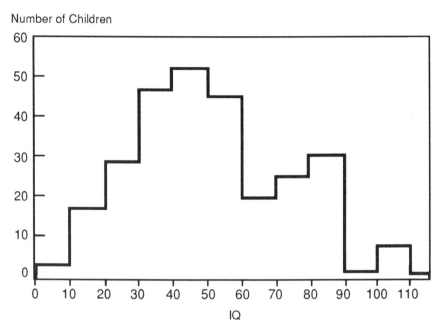

FIGURE 3.1: IQ score distribution among 260 children and young adults with autism in the study, based primarily on use of the Stanford-Binet and the WISC. Data are missing for 48 cases.

Table 3.2 shows the 11 school systems in rank order, from high to low prevalence. Note that Dallas found 5.7 children per 10,000 population, which is similar to estimates of about 5 per 10,000 from epidemiological studies that also used schools to identify the children (Wing & Gould, 1979). Interestingly, a prevalence of 10 per 10,000 was found recently in Nova Scotia where the researchers adapted the methods of Wing and Gould with broader screening criteria so that teachers referred a higher proportion of pupils to the researchers who administered standardized autism tests (Bryson et al., 1987).

TABLE 3.2

Prevalence of Autism in Children Ages 5 to 18 as Identified by the School Districts

SITE	PREVALENCE PER 10,000	SPECIAL CHARACTERISTICS
Dallas, TX	5.7	Vigorous new school screening program
Suburban Detroit, MI	2.8	State program of family stipends
Central Iowa	2.7	Many rural children in residential placement
Detroit, MI	2.6	State program of family stipends
Suburban Birmingham, AL	2.3	
Birmingham, AL	2.1	
Suffolk County, NY	1.9	
Morris County, NJ	1.9	
Fresno, CA	1.9	
Suburban and rural Fresno, CA	1.8	
Jacksonville, FL	1.2	

Why do 10 out of the 11 school systems in our study identify the prevalence of autism at less than 3 per 10,000? The factors that contribute to this low prevalence seem less related to the actual distribution of autism and more to the way schools serve these children. Autism is excluded from the federally defined categories of P.L. 94-142 under which the states identify and serve children with handicapping conditions, and although states are at liberty to use autism as a category for educational diagnosis, they rarely do.

For instance, the Morris County, NJ, special education system which classifies these children as emotionally impaired, found a prevalence of only 1.9 per 10,000. Some school systems use terms such as "autistic-like" and "autistic features," due to parental sensitivity over the term "autism." Testing is infrequent because none of the tests for autism is considered authoritative in the way that the Stanford-Binet and the WISC are authoritative in the measurement of intelligence. Finally, few districts have specific educational programs for autistic children due to the lack of consensus on the most effective and appropriate approaches to education and behavior management.

Those school systems in our sample that identified the lowest prevalence also provided the least comprehensive programs for children with autism. Experience in Dallas illustrates how the rate of autism known to the schools depends upon the schools' provision of programs. In 1983, the Dallas school system knew of one child with autism. With a vigorous screening and service program, by 1985 Dallas had identified 127 children, and by 1988 had identified and was serving 147, at a prevalence of 7 per 10,000.

According to parental reports on nine functional activities of daily living, many children and young adults needed assistance in daily routines. About 60% needed assistance in dressing themselves and about 35% in using the toilet. As would be expected, they generally had no problems in feeding themselves, walking, or climbing stairs. However, only 30% sought the company of other people and only 20% could speak so that everyone could understand.

Percent

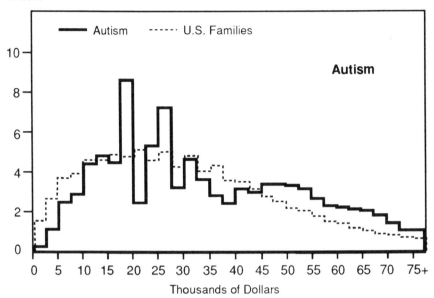

Percent

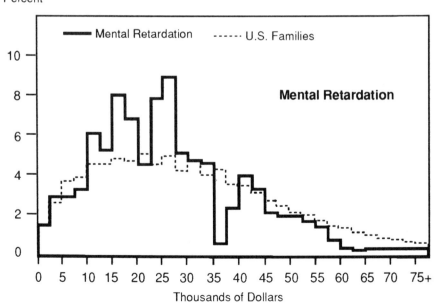

Figure 3.2: Income distribution of families in the study compared to all families in metropolitan America, 1985. National data are from the Bureau of Census (1987b.)

Almost 40% of the families of autistic children in the sample had annual incomes above $35,000, compared to only 26% of the families of severely and profoundly mentally retarded children. On the whole, the income distribution of families of children with autism has more families at the upper end than the distribution for all families living in metropolitan areas, as shown in Figure 3.2.

Severe and Profound Mental Retardation

Criteria for including children with severe or profound mental retardation in the study called for a set of measurements and other criteria that were educational rather than medical. In looking at the low end of a range of scores, in this case IQ test results, the question of a cut-off point arises.

The alternative criteria used in selecting children for the study were: (a) they scored 35 or less on a Stanford Binet or equivalent intelligence test; (b) the school system's formal decision was that they were too low functioning to test; (c) they were identified as at high risk for severe mental retardation, but were too young to test. Among the 326 severely or profoundly mentally retarded children, 41% were never tested, 38% were tested once, and 12% were given two IQ tests.

A reasonable estimate of the prevalence of severe and profound mental retardation in a school-age population seems to be between 1.0 and 1.5 per 1,000. Stein and Susser (1986) find a fairly steady prevalence over time across Western societies of about 3.4 to 4 per 1,000 for school-age children in the profound, severe, and moderate ranges, that is, those who have IQ scores of less than 50.

For convenience, they and other researchers, such as Richardson (1984), employ the term "severe" to include individuals in the moderate range, and most epidemiological studies do not separately estimate the prevalence of either severe or profound retardation (Kiernan & Bruininks, 1986). Therefore, we applied a Gaussian curve to the Stein and Susser estimate to derive our prevalence estimate.

Specifically, this probability distribution predicts that of all individuals with mental retardation, 85% are in the mild range, 10% are in the moderate range and 5% in the severe and profound ranges. Taking roughly one-third of the Stein and Susser estimate yields 1 to 1.5 per 1,000 children of school age. Due to premature death, the prevalence of severe retardation drops dramatically in the preschool years.

A British Cohort study indicated a severe mental retardation prevalence of 8.8 per 1,000 at birth and 2.6 per 1,000 at age 7, yielding a survival rate of 29% to age 7 (Hansen, Belmont, & Stein, 1980). A recent review of the role of socioeconomic status found no indication that social class factors are associated with the prevalence of severe mental retardation (Kiely, 1987).

In our study sites the prevalence of children ages 5 to 18 who were identified by the schools varied as much as the rates for identified cases of autism. The highest prevalence rate was in Jefferson County, AL, with 3.3 per 1,000, but the central city of Birmingham identified half that rate. The lowest rates were found in Morris County, NJ, Suffolk County, NY, and Jacksonville, FL, all with a prevalence of only 0.5. Possibly some children in the affluent suburban districts were served by private schools without the knowledge of the public school system, but the generally low rates warrant investigation.

Individuals with severe and profound mental retardation are a medically involved sample. In this group, 88% of the children were diagnosed under the age of two. A very high proportion of the severely mentally retarded children in the study—three out of five—had seizures. The limited physical abilities of these children and young adults were described by their parents. Only about 30% could walk half a mile and about 40% could climb ten stairs. About 80% needed assistance in dressing and about 65% in using the toilet. Only 5% could speak clearly, but 50% did seek out the company of other people.

Among those of school age, all these children were in special classes, the majority being located in special schools. Fourteen percent were in residential schools. In sum, not only were the children different within each developmental disability category, but their families differed economically, socially, and ethnically. In the next chapter we look at average uses of health care services and show how some of these differences influenced utilization.

Chapter 4

Utilization of Health Care and Medical Services

The question of who gets what services is important to answer for children with serious chronic illnesses and developmental disabilities. Children with autism and children with severe and profound mental retardation vary tremendously in their utilization of health care, such that a small proportion of the children receive a large proportion of the services. The variation is less among young adults.

Starfield and her associates (1984) have pointed out that chronically ill children at different times in their lives may not require or seek medical services. She found that most of the factors that affect a seriously chronically ill child's capacity to develop and adapt are in the health and medical service sector and have little to do with the degree of the child's functional impairment or type of disease. Starfield and Dutton (1985) advocated performing more extensive research on the delivery of clinical and health services in order to increase understanding of how to help this at-risk population.

This chapter describes utilization of health care and medical services by making comparisons with the national averages for children and young adults. The two comprehensive national data sets against which we frequently compare the developmentally disabled sample are both from the National Center for Health Statistics (NCHS, 1987): the 1986 Health Interview Survey that covered 24,000 households (NCHS 1987b) and the 1980 National Medical Care Utilization and Expenditure Survey (NMCUES) based on 6,600 households (NCHS, 1983). In the future, insightful comparisons can be made when the National Center for Health Services Research releases all the data from the 1987 National Medical Expenditure Survey (NMES).

We begin with visits to a physician, then describe hospitalizations and emergency room use, and close by examining preventive care and habilitative therapies. Variability in levels of utilization is examined in terms of demographic characteristics of the families, severity of the child's medical condition, and possession of health insurance.

All the data reported here are from the 12 month period beginning July, 1985, and ending June, 1986. They provide a cross-sectional view of the diversity of utilization patterns. Where appropriate, we discuss these data as though they were longitudinal, by assuming that in the past the young adults in the sample used services similarly to the present children. Further, we believe that tomorrow's children will use services in patterns similar to yesterday's.

VISITS TO PHYSICIANS

We begin with physicians because they are the source of primary care and gatekeepers for the health care system. Extreme variation is characteristic of American patterns in the use of physicians' services. Children with severe and profound mental retardation are at the extreme end of a range, the 3 children per 1,000 who have the most serious mental deficits. Even among these children utilization of physician services is extremely skewed. After describing the variation, we examine the extent to which the severity of the child's physical condition predicts the number of physician visits and the degree to which inequitable influences, such as income and race, affect the level of visits.

Frequency of Visits to Physicians

Children and young adults with autism visit physicians about 4 times per year, about the same as the national average of 3.6 visits for those from birth through age 24. By contrast, as can be seen in Table 4.1, children and young adults with severe retardation average about 9 visits per year.

TABLE 4.1

Average Annual Physician Visits by Age and Place of Contact

AGE AND GROUP	N	ALL VISITS	PRIVATE OFFICE	OUTPATIENT CLINIC & OTHER
0-24 years				
U.S. average	–	3.6	2.3	1.2
Autism	308	4	3	1
Severe mental retardation	326	9	6	3
Under 5 years				
U.S. average	–	5.2	3.7	1.4
Autism	24	6	4	2
Severe mental retardation	50	15	8	7
5-17 years				
U.S. average	–	2.8	1.8	1
Autism	227	4	3	1
Severe mental retardation	185	9	6	3
18-24 years				
U.S. average	–	3.8	2.2	1.6
Autism	57	4	3	1
Severe mental retardation	91	6	5	1

Note. The source of the national figures is the National Center for Health Statistics (1987b). *Current Estimates from the National Health Interview Survey, 1986,* Series 10, No. 164, p. 117. Washington, DC: Public Health Service.

An individual's annual number of physician visits is defined as the sum of all visits to physicians' offices, hospital outpatient departments, and emergency rooms. The inclusion of all clinic visits results in a small overestimate for about 10% of the sample who saw allied health care providers in outpatient departments. The average number of visits is rounded in this and most tables in order to emphasize that the figure is an estimate. The national estimate is given in decimals because it has that degree of accuracy.

Due to the great variation in averages among the sites in the study, the results in all the tables should be read as approximations. Severely and profoundly retarded children under age 5 averaged about 15 ambulatory physician visits a year, about evenly divided between physicians in private practice and hospital clinics. Among older children and into young adulthood, usage decreases with age, in contrast to the population as a whole, where an upswing begins with young adults.

Two-thirds of the children with severe retardation had physical impairments, which accounted for their high visit levels. Note that preschool children were going to hospital clinics, where specialists are available, at about five times the average rate, but going to physicians' offices at about twice the rate. We found that the ability to walk half a mile separated low users of medical services from high users. Among school-age children who could walk half a mile, the average annual number of ambulatory visits was about five and dropped to about four among young adults. For both age groups, this is half the rate of visits made by the children and young adults who could not walk half a mile.

In sum, the severely retarded children without physical impairment had visit levels similar to children with autism. The importance of this distinction between children who are physically and mentally impaired and those who are simply mentally impaired is that the higher the intellectual functioning of the child, the less the likelihood of severe physical disabilities. In the moderate range, physical disabilities occur much less frequently. Any extrapolation of our findings to children in the moderate range should adjust for the proportion who have physical disabilities.

Home versus Residential Placement

A unique feature of this study is its inclusion of children in residential placement together with children at home. Table 4.2 shows that for both mental retardation and autism, those in residential placement had higher levels of medical visits than those at home, except among autistic children, where visit levels were similar. The levels of functional ability and physical impairment were fairly similar for those at home and in placement, a finding discussed in Chapter 9.

A clear difference is that government regulations require that residential facilities to provide a minimum number of health maintenance visits for all residents. For example, Intermediate Care Facilities require all clients to have annual medical, dental, and audiological checkups so that the facility remains certified as eligible for Medicaid funding. Among children and young adults in both disability groups, we found that almost no one in a residence failed to see at least one physician during the reference year. Those at home who saw no physician during the year included about 10% of the autistic children, about 15% of the autistic adults, and about 25% of the retarded adults. The most pronounced differences are for young adults in both disability categories: those in residences have over twice as many visits as those at home.

TABLE 4.2

Variation in Physician Visits by Living Arrangements

AGE AND GROUP	AVERAGE ANNUAL PHYSICIAN VISITS			
	HOME	N	AWAY	N
0-24 years				
Autism	4	284	6	24
Severe mental retardation	8	254	10	72
5-17 years				
Autism	5	214	5	13
Severe mental retardation	8	150	10	35
18-24 years				
Autism	3	46	7	11
Severe mental retardation	4	58	10	33

Note. Because a small proportion of very young children are in residential placement, no breakdown is shown.

Age and Disability

Extreme variations in the number of ambulatory physician visits occur for both conditions. Table 4.3 compares those surveyed to national averages and illustrates that far fewer children are low users and far more are high users of physician services.

Among autistic children, the extremes include about 10% with no services, roughly another 15% with one visit and less than 2% with more than 20 visits. The children with severe retardation have even more diverse patterns, with only about 5% seeing no physicians and about 15% having more than 20 physician visits in a year. Among young adults, the variation is not quite so extreme, with fewer high users.

Race and Ethnicity

In American society, race has declined as a barrier to service, but substantial racial differences remain in utilization of health services. The 1986 data from the National Health Interview Survey show that white children under 18 had 4.5 physician contacts per year, as compared to 2.5 for black children (National Center for Health Statistics, 1987a). Interestingly, the racial differences in the general population are far smaller for adults.

TABLE 4.3

Extremes in Physician Service Use

AGE AND GROUP	N	AVERAGE ANNUAL PHYSICIAN VISITS			
		0	1	2–19	20+
Under 17 years					
U.S. average	–	20.7%	20.3%	56.7%	2.3%
Autism	226	10	15	75	<2
Severe mental retardation	223	5	5	75	15
17-24 years					
U.S. average	–	21.9	19.5	55.6	3
Autism	82	15	10	75	<1
Severe mental retardation	109	15	10	70	5

Note. National averages are from the National Center for Health Statistics. (1985). *High and low-volume users of health services, United States, 1980,* Series C, Analytical Report No. 2, p. 40. Washington, DC: Public Health Service. Study data are rounded to avoid more precision than the data warrant. The age groups are defined consistent with the published national data.

For children with developmental disabilities, Table 4.4 shows a consistent pattern across the two disabilities and age groups: white children received more physician services than Hispanic and Asian children, who received more services than black children.

In this table we show the ranges of the site averages in order to inform the reader that the overall averages presented in each table are not exact, but approximations. As explained in the chapter on methods, the bottom of the range is the average for the site which is next to the lowest among the seven metropolitan areas in the study, and the top of the range is the average for the site which has the next to the highest average. The true average for the children living in metropolitan areas is very likely to fall within the range given.

For instance, zero is the lowest number of physician visits by an individual with mental retardation and 87 in a year is the highest. Table 4.4 shows that the overall average for black individuals with severe mental retardation is 5. We show the range as running between 4 and 8 because five of the seven sites were that close together.

The convention of excluding the lowest site from the presentation of the range dropped off the average for Fresno, which was 4. The extremely high site was Des Moines, with 14. Both of these extreme sites had few black children, so chance pushed their averages exceptionally low and high. Given that our seven sites were picked in a judgment sample, the true average for all severely retarded black children and young adults in metropolitan areas may not be 5, but it is very likely to fall inside the range presented, that is, between 4 and 8.

TABLE 4.4

Variation in Physician Visits by Race and Ethnicity

AGE AND GROUP	N	AVERAGE ANNUAL PHYSICIAN VISITS			
		TOTAL N=634	WHITE N=347	HISPANIC & ASIAN N=75	BLACK N=212
0-24 years					
Autism	308	5	5	4	3
		3-5	3-6	4-5	2-3
Severe mental retardation	326	9	11	8	5
		6-11	7-13	6-12	4-8
5-17 years					
Autism	227	4	5	4	3
		3-6	3-6	3-5	2-3
Severe mental retardation	185	9	10	7	5
		5-9	5-9	5-6	4-8
18-24 years					
Autism	57	4	4	3	2
		2-6	2-6	1-3	2-3
Severe mental retardation	91	6	8	3	4
		2-7	4-11	3-3	3-5

Note. Because the sample is drawn from only seven metropolitan areas, a range of site means is presented below each estimate. This range represents the next to lowest and next to highest site means.

White individuals with severe mental retardation averaged visits from 7 to 13 at the various sites in the range we present. Jacksonville happened to be the excluded extremely low site, with 5 visits. Fresno, at 16, had the extreme high not shown in the range. For all three racial groups, the overall average we calculated falls neatly within the range, permitting us to conclude that the difference we found between 5 visits for black children and 11 for white reflects a true difference.

The purpose of showing the range is to assist the reader to imagine what the results would be if other sites were drawn to represent American children. If so, the averages might differ by a visit or two, but they would very likely fall within the ranges we show. A very cautious interpretation of the data is that the average number of visits for black individuals could be as high as 7 or 8 and the average number of visits for white individuals could be as low as 7 or 8. However, finding a similar pattern among both children and young adults in both disability groups suggests the less conservative interpretation, that racial disparities exist in the frequency of physician visits.

Ranges are useful in another way. They can be used as a correction when the overall average is pulled high by a few extreme outliers. For example, white school-age children who are mentally retarded are shown with an overall mean of 10 visits but the range runs from 5 to 9. This result occurred because one site had a very high average, 18, pulling the overall average above the range of the five intermediate sites. A reasonable interpretation is that the true mean is somewhere between 5 and 10. In general, the smaller the number of cases, the more likely are the results to produce a wide range that is not centered on the overall average.

Researchers studying health care seeking behavior have pointed to the mother's educational attainment as an important enabling factor, determining whether children receive health services, particularly those of the preventive kind (Andersen, Lion, Anderson, 1976). In our findings, better educated mothers were more likely to name a pediatrician as the child's regular source of care and less likely to name a general practitioner than less educated women, and among the families of autistic children, the relationship is even stronger than for the sample as a whole. For children with severe retardation, the more educated the mother, the more physician visits the child made.

Insurance Coverage

Economic barriers continue to be major problems in providing adequate care for the general population. In national probability studies, authors often examine how income, insurance coverage, or other enabling factors impact on the utilization of services. The data we collected show a strong relationship between financing and utilization: Health care is more likely to be acquired if there is some insurance coverage. Tables 4.5 and 4.6 show the variation in physician visits according to the type of insurance coverage.

Although the numbers are small for some types of insurance coverage, the data on children are shown separately because of the huge drop in private coverage and increase in public coverage when people with developmental disabilities reach adulthood. If children and adults were combined, the higher visit levels for children would give the impression that private insurance coverage promotes higher use of services than public coverage, which is not the case. With either type of insurance, use is about the same.

Among autistic children, the least frequent users of physician services, lacked insurance coverage, as shown in the top row of Table 4.5. Overall, about one quarter had no visits, although the range of 0 to 49% shows that in some sites none of the uninsured children went without visits and in others almost half did. Among children with either public or private insurance, about 10% had no visits, and among those with both public and private coverage, about 1% had no visits.

TABLE 4.5

Autism: Variation in Annual Physician Visits by Type of Insurance Coverage

INSURANCE	N	% OF GROUP BY LEVEL OF VISITS			
		0	1-5	6-19	20+
Under 18 years					
None	18	24%	60%	15%	0
		0-49	51-79	0-21	–
Private	138	9	58	29	4
		2-14	37-86	12-46	0-3
Public	63	9	63	23	5
		0-13	41-69	9-36	0-14
Private and	32	1	84	15	0
public		0-0	47-100	0-53	–
18-24 years					
None	1	100	0	0	0
		–	–	–	–
Private	8	0	89	11	0
		–	53-100	0-47	–
Public	22	19	60	22	0
		0-50	31-100	0-64	–
Private and	26	9	56	35	0
public		0-0	50-100	0-40	–

Note. Because the sample is drawn from only seven metropolitan areas, a range of site means is presented below each estimate. The range represents the next to the lowest and next to highest site percentages.

Table 4.6 shows that severely retarded individuals with some insurance coverage were more likely to have high use (6 to 19 visits) and extremely high use (20 and above). Whether the coverage is only private, only public, or a combination of both makes little difference.

Appropriateness of the Volume of Physician Visits

To what extent is the wide variation in the children's number of physician visits based directly on medical need? Similarly, what are the influences of the family's racial background, finances, and education level on medical usage? To assess the effect of socioeconomic variables on use of physician services, we conducted a substudy of the 152 autistic and 191 severely retarded individuals living at home whose primary physicians had supplied data on their patient's diagnoses and chronic medical conditions.

Members of a panel of pediatricians specializing in developmental disabilities made independent judgments based on the survey data from the parents and the report from the primary physician concerning etiology and chronic conditions. The method has three steps, which were discussed in chapter 2.

TABLE 4.6

Severe and Profound Mental Retardation: Variation in Annual Physician Visits by Type of Insurance Coverage

INSURANCE	N	% OF GROUP BY LEVEL OF VISITS			
		0	1-5	6-19	20+
Under 18 years					
None	11	18%	64%	18%	0%
		0-20	50-100	0-20	–
Private	82	4	43	43	11
		0-4	33-67	29-68	0-14
Public	78	4	33	45	18
		0-6	23-100	0-54	0-30
Private and	64	8	27	50	16
Public		0-13	13-33	33-57	0-25
18-24 years					
None	1	0	100	0	0
		–	–	–	–
Private	3	33	33	33	
		0-0	0-0	0-0	–
Public	55	26	42	27	6
		0-40	25-63	0-43	0-0
Private and	32	19	34	44	3
public		0-25	17-67	33-56	0-0

Note. Below each mean percentage is the range representing the next to lowest and next to highest site percentages. The range 0-0 indicates that only the highest site percentage exceeded 0.

First, we developed algorithms that set a minimum annual number of physician visits appropriate for monitoring each chronic condition of the child. Second, we compared and made consistent the criteria for the algorithms. Third, we reviewed the cases so as to take into account instances where coordinated care would reduce the total number of appropriate visits to a number less than the one produced by the algorithms.

The annual number of visits recommended by the panel ranged from 1.8 to 19. Among the autistic population, the most common reasons for additional physician visits were to monitor seizure disorders and medication levels, and to arrange hospital admissions and discharges. For children with severe retardation, the variety of congenital disorders requiring increased physician visits included orthopedic impairments, seizures, hearing loss, vision problems,

heart defects and gastrointestinal problems, with some of these disorders requiring hospital admissions. The most severely involved child was estimated
to require a minimum of 18 ambulatory visits.

Multivariate analysis showed that the severity of the condition was by far
the most influential determinant of the number of physician visits. When the
analysis took the severity of the child's condition into account, the results
showed that socioeconomic characteristics also influenced the actual number
of visits. In families where the mother had a part-time job, the visit level was
higher than where she was employed full-time and where she was not
employed.

Children with autism were more likely to lack the appropriate level of
physician visits if they came from disadvantaged backgrounds. The simple
odds ratio used here is how many times more likely a disadvantaged child
is to have too few physician visits than a child with advantages. It is computed by dividing the odds of not having an appropriate number of physician visits among those in the risk group by the odds of not having an
appropriate number of physician visits among those in the reference group.
Table 4.7 shows that five different characteristics increased the odds that a child
would not receive sufficient monitoring visits.

TABLE 4.7

**Autism: The Odds for Children Living at Home to Lack Appropriately
Frequent Care from Physicians**

CHARACTERISTIC	N	% NOT RECEIVING APPROPRIATELY FREQUENT CARE	SIMPLE ODDS RATIO
Race			
Nonwhite	35	29%	3.7
White	72	10	
Urban			
City	37	24	2.3
Suburb	70	12	
Poverty			
Below 300%	58	22	2.9
300% & above	49	9	
Mother's level of education			
≤2 years college	73	21	6.5
>2 years college	34	4	
Parent must take time off from work for health visits			
Yes	28	24	2.8
No	51	10	

Note. The simple odds ratio is how many times more likely a disadvantaged child is to have too
few physician visits than a child with advantages. For example, the odds for a nonwhite child
to lack visits .29/(1−.29) = .408. For a white child the odds are .1/(1−.1) = .111. The ratio of the
odds for a nonwhite compared to a white child is .408/.111 = 3.7.

Twenty-nine percent of the black, Hispanic, and Asian children had too few physician visits compared to 10% of the white children. The odds for a minority child to lack appropriate care were about 3.7 times higher than for a white child. Children living in a central city were twice as likely to lack physician visits. If a minority family lived in a central city, the disadvantage is compounded. Lower family income also set the odds against children. During the study year of 1985, the poverty line for a family of four was $10,903. Those who had incomes below 300% of poverty are three times more likely to have a shortfall in visits. Mother's education was the most powerful predictor, resulting in odds against children whose mothers had less than two years of college of over 6 to 1. Furthermore, parents who had to take time off from work for their child's medical visits had odds of 2.8 for shortfalls in visits.

The picture is similar for young adults with autism, and statistically significant despite the fact that only 34 were in this substudy. Those from modest and low income families, here pegged at less than 250% of poverty, were 10 times more likely to have an inadequate number of physician visits. The mother being single had a similar effect. Lacking Medicaid coverage raised the odds of lacking physician visits for these young adults, but did not influence the odds for autistic children or for individuals with severe retardation, possibly because there was so little variance; very few of the autistic children have Medicaid coverage and few of the severely retarded offspring lacked it.

For children with severe retardation, unexpected findings emerged from comparing the actual number of visits to the number of monitoring visits recommended by the pediatric specialists in developmental disabilities. The severely retarded offspring of more affluent and married mothers were less likely to have sufficient visits than children of poorer and single mothers. Where the family income was above $20,000, children were about four times less likely to have appropriate visit levels than children in poorer families.

Our analyses found no influence on visit level from the number of insurance policies, central city residence, mother's employment, or the child's race. The basic explanation is that Medicaid coverage was a significant influence on whether or not these children had an appropriate number of visits to physicians. The influence of Medicaid shows in the ability of single parents to reach the appropriate visit level more frequently than married parents. We found that children in two-parent families for whom the physician panel recommended between 1 and 4 monitoring visits in fact averaged 4 visits for monitoring plus acute care, but those in single-parent families averaged 7 visits.

The pattern is reversed when we look at the 18-24-year-old group. Adults with severe mental retardation were much more likely to have appropriate visit levels when the mothers were married and the family income was above $30,000. Many of these adults were supported by Supplemental Security Income (SSI), the income maintenance program for the fully disabled that is managed by the Social Security Administration, which in most states automatically creates Medicaid eligibility. Coverage by Medicaid was 90% among severely retarded young adults, and thus its presence does not account for adequate visit levels.

HOSPITAL CARE

The annual number of short-term hospital stays is a standard measure of health care utilization. Not only does hospitalization indicate the presence of a serious medical condition in the child, but also it is the major health care expenditure on behalf of American children despite its rare occurrence. The children in our study who lived at home were more frequent users of inhospital care than the average child. Table 4.8 shows that about 10% of the children with autism in the 5 to 17 age group were hospitalized during a year, compared to 3% of all children.

TABLE 4.8

Distribution of Children and Young Adults Living at Home by
Annual Short-Stay Hospital Episodes

AGE AND GROUP	N	% OF GROUP BY LEVEL OF HOSPITAL STAYS			
		0	1	2	≥3
5-17 years					
U.S. average	–	97%	2.7%	0.2%	0.1%
Autism	227	90	10	<1	0
Severe mental retardation	185	75	15	5	5
	N	0	1	≥2	
18-24 years					
U.S. average	–	95	4.4	0.7	
Autism	57	85	15	<1	
Severe mental retardation	91	85	15	<2	

Note. The national data are from the National Center for Health Statistics (1987a). *Current Estimates from the National Health Interview Survey, 1986.* Series 10, No. 164, p. 121. The national statistics exclude hospitalizations for childbirth. Study results have been rounded for presentation.

While we believe these findings are accurate, the reader should be cautious in looking at these differences. We found wide variation in the ranges from site to site when aggregating hospital utilization data because of the fact that hospitalization is a rare event in comparison to, for example, doctor's visits. The contrast is more striking for children with severe mental retardation, of whom about 25% were hospitalized.

Children under age 5 are omitted from the table because the small number in our sample provides uncertain estimates. When we examine the rates of hospital utilization for the 18 to 24-year-olds sampled, the table shows an increase for young adults with autism, largely attributable to more frequent psychiatric hospitalizations. The decrease among young adults with severe retardation may be due to the completion of corrective surgery during childhood and also to higher mortality among those most severely physically impaired. For the rare families with three or more episodes of hospitalization in a year, the hospital experience becomes part of the way of life.

TABLE 4.9

Hospital Discharge Rates and Average Lengths of Stay

AGE AND GROUP	N	DISCHARGES PER 1,000	AVERAGE STAY IN DAYS
5-17 years			
U.S. average		38	4.2
Autism	227	100	6
Severe mental retardation	185	400	7
18-24 years			
U.S. average		118	4.0
Autism	57	200	15
Severe mental retardation	91	200	9

Note. National data are from the National Center for Health Statistics, 1986 hospital discharge survey, unpublished. Study results have been rounded for presentation.

Another measure of hospital use is based on the frequency of hospital discharges per 1,000 people in the population, shown in Table 4.9. The discharge rate in 1986 for all American children, ages 5 to 17, was 38 per 1,000, but for children with autism it was about 100 and for children with severe retardation about 400, due to the high incidence of comorbidity. The national discharge rate rises threefold from childhood to young adulthood, but for autism it doubles. Most of this rise can be accounted for by stays in psychiatric hospitals.

By contrast, between severely retarded children and young adults, the discharge rate is roughly cut in half. The drop may be due both to completion of corrective surgery performed in childhood and to the better health of the children who survive to adulthood. The average length of a hospital stay approximated the national average of 4.2 days for children in both disability categories.

Children of mothers with only a high school education had longer than average stays. Young adults with developmental disabilities had a much longer average length of stay. Among young adults with autism, the length of stay approximated the rates for adults who undergo psychiatric hospitalization. Within this group of 15 admissions, we found the longest stay at 44 days, which pushed the average up to about 15 days.

We compared children ages 5 to 17 living at home to their age-mates in residential placement. Although the samples described were too small to provide precision, they showed that the rate of hospitalization for individuals in residential settings was not far above the rates for those living at home, unlike the rates of ambulatory care, which were much higher for children in placement (See Table 4.2).

EMERGENCY ROOM USE

A comparison of rates of utilization of emergency rooms between children with autism and those with severe and profound mental retardation indicates not only the amount of resources that are expended but also what stresses are placed on families when managing these conditions. A question to explore is whether or not some of these emergency room visits could be eliminated through case management programs that emphasize prophylaxes, such as antiseizure medication.

Our estimates for frequency of emergency room use are less accurate than those for hospitalizations, due to the difficulty of distinguishing services in emergency rooms from other outpatient department services. Our conservative estimation procedure is described in Chapter 2.

TABLE 4.10

Autism: Emergency Room (ER) Use by Children and Young Adults Living at Home

CHARACTERISTIC	N	% OF GROUP AT VARIOUS VISIT LEVELS		
		0	1	2 OR MORE
Age[a]				
Under 18 years	238	75%	15%	10%
18-24 years	46	80	<20	>0
Race[a]				
White	134	80	10	10
Black	120	75	20	5
Hispanic and Asian	30	70	25	5
Income[b]				
<$17,386	92	70	15	15
17,387-35,000	91	75	20	5
≥35,001	101	85	10	5
Poverty[c]				
<300%	189	70	20	10
≥300%	95	90	>5	<5

Note. Results have been rounded for presentation.
[a]Not significant.
[b]$p < .05$. [c]$p < .001$.

Fourteen percent of all American children living at home visited an emergency room at least once during 1980, and 2.4% visited the ER twice or more (Public Health Service, 1983). For the sake of comparison, our data reported in Tables 4.10 and 4.11 also concern only children living at home.

Children with autism had substantially higher visit levels than the average child, 15% having at least one trip to the ER and roughly 10% with more than one visit. Emergency room usage seems not to drop for the young adults, probably because unpredictable and dangerous actions do not abate with age.

Nationally, children from minority groups use emergency rooms more frequently than white children, but we found no statistically significant difference in this population. Autistic children from higher income families visit emergency rooms less often than those from middle and low income families, as in the American population at large.

Table 4.11 shows a substantial drop in visits after childhood among those with severe mental retardation, again like the American population at large. In both disability categories, individuals with seizures were more likely to visit emergency rooms than those who had never had seizures. Of the autistic children, adolescents, and young adults who had experienced more than 100 seizures in their lifetime, about 40% went to the emergency room at least once during the year under study, compared to about 15% of those who were free of seizures.

TABLE 4.11

Severe and Profound Mental Retardation: Emergency Room (ER) Use by Children and Young Adults Living at Home

		% OF GROUP AT VARIOUS VISIT LEVELS		
CHARACTERISTIC	N	0	1	2 OR MORE
Age^a				
Under 18 years	196	75%	15%	10%
18-24 years	58	90	>5	<5
$Race^b$				
White	144	80	15	5
Black	74	75	15	10
Hispanic and Asian	36	75	15	<10
$Income^b$				
<$17,386	99	70	20	10
$17,387-35,000	95	80	15	5
≥$35,001	60	85	<10	<5
$Poverty^a$				
<300%	189	75	>15	<10
≥300%	65	85	>10	<5

Note. Results have been rounded for presentation.
[a]$p < .05$.
[b]Not significant.

PREVENTIVE SERVICES AND
HABILITATIVE THERAPIES

For all children periodic medical and dental examinations are a wise investment. For children with developmental disabilities any of a wide range of therapeutic services may also be appropriate. For parents, genetic counseling may be able to inform them of their risk of having another severely developmentally disabled child and quiet their fears in planning for subsequent births.

Genetic Counseling

Professional advice on the genetics of disability was received by about half of the parents of children with autism and children with severe or profound mental retardation. Higher family income and being white predicted whether or not parents would receive genetic advice. Among families of autistic children, those lacking health insurance rarely received genetic counseling, while those with case management usually did. However, only about 5% of all parents had received genetic counseling before the birth of their disabled child.

Routine Physical Examinations

The higher frequency of physician visits for children with developmental disabilities than for children at large does not assure that they will receive timely physical examinations, because they often see subspecialists. In our survey, parents and other primary caretakers responded to the question, "What is the month and year of the last time (Johnny) went for a checkup?" Our results showed that only about 70% of the children up to age 6 in both disability groups were meeting the American Academy of Pediatrics standard, which recommends an annual physical examination. For those age 7 to 20, where the standard is biennial, about 85% of the 223 autistic youth and about 95% of the 203 severely retarded youth met the standard.

Dental Visits

Time elapsed since the last dental visit is a measure of the regularity of care received by children. While few American children have acute problems with their teeth and gums, dental care is considered a major component of children's health service in every major industrialized nation. The results in Table 4.12 support the hypothesis that children with severe developmental disabilities do not see a dentist as frequently as other children.

The American Dental Association standard of visits annually, or more often if indicated, was met by only about 60% of the children in both disability groups. For children and young adults with severe mental retardation from birth through age 24, about 85% of those in residential placement had been to a dentist within the last year, compared to about 55% of those living with their families. In fact, about 20% of the children with mental retardation living at home had never been checked by a dentist, compared to about 2% of those living away from their families.

TABLE 4.12

Elapsed Time Since Last Dental Visit

AGE AND GROUP	% MORE THAN 1 YEAR	N
5-17 years		
U.S. average	28	–
Autism	40	221
Severe mental retardation	40	182
18-24 years		
U.S. average	42	–
Autism	25	56
Severe mental retardation	45	90

Note. U.S. data are from the National Center for Health Statistics (1987b). *Current Estimates from the National Health Interview Survey, 1986,* Series 10, No. 164, p. 10. Washington, DC: Public Health Service. Study results have been rounded for presentation.

Frequently, children with autism refuse to cooperate with a dentist and are unwilling even to sit in the dental chair. One mother told us of taking her son five times to the dental office but failing each time to gain his cooperation. The dental problems of these children grow worse until they are finally admitted to a hospital for dental work while anesthetized.

Specific insurance coverage for dental care is a relatively new benefit both in private and public insurance. The length of time between dental visits varies according to whether there is insurance coverage for dental care. For those children covered by Medicaid who lived in states where Medicaid did not cover dental services, the length of time between dental visits was several years. This result captures succinctly the way in which the utilization of preventive services is affected by financial concerns.

Habilitative Therapies

Services to habilitate and rehabilitate individuals suffering from chronic conditions are not well provided and financed by the American health care system. Among the tens of thousands of children with severe developmental disabilities, many would benefit from habilitative therapies. Children with autism and children with severe and profound mental retardation are underserved, as measured by both retrospective parental reports and concurrent physician recommendations.

We asked the parents, "Has a physician *ever* told you that (CHILD) should get treatment from a speech, physical, occupational or some other kind of therapist?" The question asked the parents to recall a physician judgment in order to have an expert opinion on the needs of each child. The sum of their recollections is that about half had been recommended some form of therapy. Of those receiving recommendations, 88% of the parents of autistic children and 75% of the parents of children with mental retardation recalled following the recommendation.

A different view of the need for therapies comes from physicians. For each child who had a usual source of health care for his or her disability, we asked the child's physician, "In your judgment, is physical or occupational therapy appropriate for this patient?" The 200 physicians who provided judgments considered that 75% of the children and young adults with autism and 70% of the children and young adults with severe or profound mental retardation would benefit from some physical or occupational therapy, shown in Table 4.13. However, physical therapists outside the schools were currently treating only 5% of the patients with autism and only about 30% of the patients with severe mental retardation for whom such treatment was deemed appropriate.

TABLE 4.13

Proportion of Children who Receive Appropriate Therapies Outside of School

THERAPY	AUTISM	N	SEVERE MENTAL RETARDATION	N
Occupational/Physical % of children who would benefit	75%	152	70%	191
% of children who would benefit that received OT/PT	<5	82	30	122
Speech % of children who would benefit	65	152	40	191
% of children who would benefit that received speech therapy	<10	84	<15	71

Note. Results have been rounded for presentation.

Although the research design we employed did not permit us to identify whether children were receiving physical or occupational therapy in school, we believe that few were. Palfrey and her colleagues (1990) in their study of five cities found that only 7% of children in special education received these therapies through the schools. Among children with emotional problems (the category where children with autism are often inappropriately placed), 3% received services and 19% of the children with retardation received services.

These figures suggest that it is unlikely that as many as half the children in our study received services at school, a level necessary to come near the physicians' judgment of need.

A similarly bleak picture emerged for speech therapy, unless the schools were providing it. From the five-city study we note that schools provided speech therapy to 25% of the children with emotional problems and to 57% of children with mental retardation. Physicians judged that two-thirds of their patients with autism would benefit from speech therapy, but less than 10% received it. From the roughly 40% of the patients with severe retardation judged able to benefit, less than 15% received speech therapy.

Physicians' judgments that physical or occupational therapy was appropriate were spread evenly across race, mother's marital status, and mother's education. Being younger and living at home increased the likelihood that the physician would recommend physical therapy.

Why does the discrepancy occur that about 80% of parents overall recalled following a physician's recommendation for therapy, but Table 4.13 shows that only about 10% of the patients were receiving therapy that physicians considered appropriate? Some of the difference lies in the methods of obtaining data.

TABLE 4.14

The Odds for Severely and Profoundly Retarded Children to Lack Physical Therapy outside of School Despite Medical Judgment that They Would Benefit

GROUP	N	% NOT RECEIVING PHYSICAL THERAPY	SIMPLE ODDS RATIO
Living arrangement			
Home	90	75%	5
Away	32	40	
Age			
≥ 10 years	69	85	4
< 10 years	53	55	
Poverty			
< 250%	57	80	3
≥ 250%	62	60	
Private insurance			
Lack	40	85	3
Have	82	65	

Note. Results have been rounded for presentation.

On the one hand, the theory of cognitive dissonance holds that parents who did not follow physicians' advice would tend to forget it, and hence their recall of following advice is too optimistic. On the other hand, it is too pessimistic to compare our estimation of actual services to what the physicians told us. The proportion of physicians who actually recommended therapy to the parents was probably lower than the proportion who gave this judgment to us as researchers. In conclusion, we believe that less than half of the study population who could have benefitted from therapies were actually receiving them.

Access to services may sometimes be due to the existence of rules and regulations related to care. Table 4.14 explains which characteristics increased an individual's chances of actually receiving physical or occupational therapy.

This table shows that, for the children who could benefit, the likelihood of receiving therapy was highest for those in residential placement. The impact of policy is clear since physician monitoring is mandatory and Medicaid pays for physical therapy in most states outside the South, which in our sample is three of the eight states. That age predicts usage is highly appropriate, but inequities appear in the strong odds working against poorer children and those lacking private insurance.

CONCLUSIONS

Health care for children with autism is not greatly different from the average child, except for slightly more frequent hospitalizations and the pronounced need for habilitative therapies. Among children with severe or profound retardation, there is a wide range in the need for services. It runs from one visit a year for monitoring development to repeated hospitalizations and dozens of ambulatory physician visits. Within this diversity, some characteristics that predict health care use in the population at large also hold true for these disabled children. Black children are less likely to receive medical attention than white children. Lack of insurance coverage predicts lower health care usage. The mother's educational attainment also predicts higher use of preventive and habilitative care and lower use of emergency room services. This diversity in utilization is the foundation for the diversity in expenditures, discussed in the next chapter.

Chapter 5

_____Expenditures

Parents rarely expect to have to deal with the disappointments and concerns for the present and the future that are associated with serious chronic illness in children. These illnesses, which can be characterized by a great deal of corrective surgery and other interventions, prolonged care over a lifetime, and possibly progressive degeneration, require constant parental involvement. To compensate for the disability, parents must become exceptionally active in promoting their children's welfare. At the same time that this social and psychological mobilization on behalf of the seriously chronically ill child is occurring, the family is facing unexpected financial burdens.

In this chapter we explore the differences in expenditure patterns among the two developmental disabilities under study and make appropriate comparisons to children in national probability studies. Because some individuals in the study lived in foster care, group homes, and other institutional settings, we compare their expenditure patterns with those living at home, controlling for differences in level of severity. Along with examining the expenses for inpatient and outpatient care from a variety of sources, we determine how much per capita was spent on a broad range of services such as allied health professionals, drugs, equipment, and supplies. Finally, we examine a wide variety of expenses that families incur to keep their son or daughter at home: child care, respite care, summer programs, and home modifications.

Due to the broad definition of developmental disabilities, which includes diseases with early onset that affect the person's ability to learn and develop, children so diagnosed are diverse in their health care needs as well as in their patterns of behavior and likely development. As described in Chapter 4, in both study groups these individuals vary in restrictions on ambulation and the presence of comorbidities, such as seizures. Consequently, even where the primary condition is not responsive to medical treatment, health care services may be required to deal with other health-related problems.

OVERALL EXPENDITURE
PATTERNS

Indeed, we found a pattern of expenditures that matched the differences in utilization. Average annual total expenditures for basic medical and other health care—including hospital charges, doctors' fees, emergency room visits, and dental charges—were four times greater for children with severe mental retardation ($4,000) than for children with autism ($1,000), as shown in Table 5.1.

TABLE 5.1

Average Annual Health Care Expenditures by Living Arrangements, 1985-86

	EXPENDITURES ($ IN '000)				
AGE AND GROUP	U.S. AVERAGE[a]	AUTISM	N	SEVERE MENTAL RETARDATION	N
Under 18 years					
Home	$0.4	$1.0	238	$4.0	196
Away	NA	1.0	13	5.0	39
18-24 years					
Home	0.8	1.5	46	4.0	58
Away	NA	3.0	11	2.0	33

[a]The U.S. averages are not strictly comparable because the breakdowns available in print apply to under age 17 and ages 17 to 44. U.S. averages are based on the 1980 NMCUES Survey, adjusted upward to reflect the increase in the Consumer Price Index for Medical Care; National Center for Health Statistics (1986). *Costs of Illness: United States, 1980,* Series C, Analytical Report No. 3. Washington DC: Public Health Service.

It is useful to compare these results with findings from national probability surveys. While the National Medical Expenditure Survey data become fully available for use by scholars and the general public, initial comparisons with the findings of the 1980 survey are helpful in understanding the full impact of the health care needs of these two categories of developmental disability on families, private insurance, and public programs.

The 1980 National Medical Care Utilization and Expenditure Survey [NMCUES] (National Center for Health Statistics, 1983) provided detailed information on many items similar to those found in our study. Conducted by sampling 6,600 households including more than 17,000 people, this survey requested that participants keep records of visits and expenditures on a special calendar and obtained the data from them through quarterly interviews. Within the larger sample of 17,000 people, a sample of 6,245 persons younger than 21 were interviewed directly or through proxies.

The major way of differentiating between children with few health problems and those who suffered from chronic or serious acute illnesses was through asking respondents about the consequences in ordinary activities of childhood, including absence from school or missing playtime. For adolescent members of the sample, the researchers also asked about missing work due to health problems. In this way, the health care expenditures of children with no restrictions on the ordinary activities of childhood could be compared with children with such limitations.

Out of the 6,245 individuals under the age of 21, only 249 were identified as having major limitations on their activities. The low prevalence of many serious chronic conditions does not permit using that data set to study the health care of the types of children in our study. Moreover, the 1980 survey excluded all people living in institutions, and it did not collect data from providers and payers, but relied upon the families to keep their medical bills for the interviewers to check.

A second caveat must be stated when we compare the study data with that collected and presented by the National Center for Health Statistics. The U.S. averages are not strictly comparable because the breakdowns available in print apply to age groups 0-16 and 17-44. Moreover, the U.S. average expenditures are based on the year 1980 and are adjusted upward here to reflect increases by 1985-86 in the Consumer Price Index for Medical Care. These minor limitations aside, the 1980 NMCUES data are immensely useful as a base against which to compare our findings. Table 5.1 shows that expenditures for children with severe mental retardation were about 10 times greater than for the average American child.

To what extent were expenditures in each disability category distributed the same way as in the national probability study? The next two tables show the cumulative percentages of children who had expenses up to specific dollar amounts.

As in Chapter 4, we note that because of the site diversity, the range is often quite large. The true mean for all U.S. metropolitan areas may not be identical to the mean of our sample, yet it is extremely likely to be within the range of site means. This imprecision results from the sampling design as discussed in Chapter 2.

TABLE 5.2

Autism: Percentage with Health Care Expenditures under Specific Amounts

CHARACTERISTIC	CUMULATIVE PERCENT WITH ANNUAL EXPENDITURES					
	<$100	<$200	<$500	<$1,000	<$3,000	<$5,000
Total	15%	29%	50%	77%	93%	96%
Living Place						
Home	16	32	52	79	94	97
	12-24	26-39	44-61	71-88	90-100	96-100
Away	2	8	27	57	87	87
	0-2	0-19	13-69	59-100	100-100	100-100
Age in years						
Under 5	5	9	41	71	100	100
	0-9	0-23	7-100	54-100	100-100	100-100
5-17	16	31	51	77	93	97
	13-22	26-38	44-64	70-84	87-100	95-100

continued on next page

TABLE 5.2 *(continued)*

Autism: Percentage with Health Care Expenditures under Specific Amounts

CHARACTERISTIC	CUMULATIVE PERCENT WITH ANNUAL EXPENDITURES					
	<$100	<$200	<$500	<$1,000	<$3,000	<$5,000
≥18	15	29	49	79	90	92
	0-43	0-75	4-75	60-100	89-100	93-100
Sex						
Male	15	28	52	77	92	96
	10-19	24-36	29-65	66-82	83-100	96-100
Female	14	32	42	78	96	97
	0-20	12-53	15-72	63-100	92-100	92-100
Race						
White	15	28	45	75	91	95
	10-22	22-33	33-55	67-80	89-100	95-100
Nonwhite	15	33	61	82	97	99
	8-18	22-42	56-76	75-89	91-100	100-100
Urban						
City	17	37	57	87	95	99
	9-28	27-51	51-64	80-91	93-100	97-100
Suburban	13	23	44	68	91	93
	8-29	23-29	29-53	56-74	93-100	96-100
Poverty						
<199%	20	36	62	77	90	96
<$21,700	16-25	28-39	48-72	65-86	84-100	93-100
200-299%	17	36	58	88	97	100
$21,700-32,699	7-39	13-72	39-72	80-100	93-100	100-100
300-499%	17	29	47	81	93	95
$32,700-54,499	0-23	9-46	9-57	67-100	93-100	100-100
≥500%	5	18	32	58	89	91
$54,500+	0-6	0-36	6-59	40-75	94-100	98-100
Insurance						
None	28	30	51	95	100	100
	12-58	12-58	38-100	96-100	100-100	100-100
Private	12	29	45	76	94	97
	7-25	15-44	40-56	68-91	93-100	99-100
Public	15	27	46	70	91	96
	0-19	0-29	19-64	58-79	77-100	81-100
Both	16	31	68	83	90	91
	0-33	0-63	38-100	73-100	92-100	94-100

Note. The ranges show the percentages at the next to the lowest and the next to the highest sites.

Tables 5.2 and 5.3 give cumulative percentages running from left to right. About 16% of the children with autism who live at home have annual medical expenditures under $100, but the wide range of 12% to 24% suggests that perhaps as many as 20% might spend less than $100. For spending that does not exceed $5,000, there is more uniformity among sites, shown by the narrow range of 96-100%.

Children and young adults in residential placement have a substantially higher pattern of expenditures than children at home. A few young adults have high expense incurred largely through psychiatric hospital stays. Families with low income tend to spend less, and those lacking insurance have a lower expenditure curve, with about one quarter spending less than $100. Sex, race, and place of residence do not show much difference across the range of expenditures.

Similar internal variations in expenditures are encountered in Table 5.3 for children with severe mental retardation, with one important difference. Owing to the presence of life-threatening comorbidities, expenditures were more likely to exceed $5,000 for children with severe mental retardation under the age of five. These birth defects often can be surgically repaired early in life or need frequent treatment.

TABLE 5.3

Severe and Profound Mental Retardation: Percentage with Health Care Expenditures under Specific Amounts

CHARACTERISTIC	CUMULATIVE PERCENT WITH ANNUAL EXPENDITURES					
	<$100	<$200	<$500	<$1,000	<$3,000	<$5,000
Total	10%	15%	25%	40%	70%	80%
Living Place						
Home	10	20	25	45	70	80
Away	5	15	20	35	65	75
Age						
Under 5	0	5	5	15	45	60
5-17	5	15	25	45	65	80
18-24	20	30	35	60	85	90
Sex						
Male	10	20	25	50	70	80
Female	10	15	25	40	70	80
Walk ½ Mile						
Cannot	5	10	15	30	60	75
Can	20	35	50	75	95	95
Race						
White	5	10	20	40	65	75
Nonwhite	20	30	40	55	75	85
Urban						
City	15	20	25	50	75	85
Suburban	5	15	25	40	65	80

continued on next page

TABLE 5.3 *(continued)*

Severe and Profound Mental Retardation: Percentage with Health Care Expenditures under Specific Amounts

CHARACTERISTIC	CUMULATIVE PERCENT WITH ANNUAL EXPENDITURES					
	<$100	<$200	<$500	<$1,000	<$3,000	<$5,000
Poverty						
Below 100% <$10,900	20	30	45	65	80	85
100-199% $10,900-21,699	10	20	30	45	75	85
200-299% $21,700-32,699	10	15	20	40	65	80
300-499% $32,700-54,499	5	5	15	40	65	85
≥500% $54,500+	5	15	25	35	65	70
Insurance						
None	5	55	65	75	85	95
Private	5	5	15	40	60	75
Public	15	25	35	45	70	80
Both	5	5	20	45	75	90

Note. The results have been rounded for presentation.

A very important finding of the study is that there are no children or young adults with autism or severe retardation whose annual medical expenses totaled more than $50,000. The most costly child among those with autism received $44,000 dollars in health care services, and the next most costly, $22,000. Among the children with severe retardation, the greatest expenses totaled $43,000 and a few others were in the upper $30,000 range.

Other studies have shown that severely disabled infants often have high expenditures for surgeries. This study included only one child in the first year of life, and only 5% of the sample was under the age of 4. Our study suggests that even those children who have extraordinary expenses in infancy, will not continue to be among the extreme outliers in the consumption of health care services. The policy implication of the absence of children whose annual expenses are in the $100,000 range is that the total cost of serving all of these children is manageable.

EXPENDITURES FOR SPECIFIC SERVICES

Expenditure patterns that reflect different service needs are found in Tables 5.4 and 5.5, where the charges for each type of health service are compared by age group across disabilities. Note what a large proportion of the expenses are accounted for by hospital bills, and what a small proportion by dental services. Comparing the two charts, we see that average expenditures for autism are about the same, in both age groups except for hospital stays, which might be artificially high because chance brought into the study a few young adults with long stays. Expenses drop for adults with severe retardation in almost every category except hospital stays.

TABLE 5.4

Average Annual Expenses for Specific Health Services: Children under Age 18

SERVICES	AUTISM $N=259$	SEVERE MENTAL RETARDATION $N=239$
Hospital	$ 300	$1,400
Physicians during hospital stays	50	375
Physicians in private practice	150	550
Outpatient	150	400
Dentists	50	25
Allied health professionals	150	400
Drugs	100	200
Equipment	20	300
Supplies	50	350
TOTAL	$1,000	$4,000

Note. Results have been rounded for presentation.

For purposes of comparison and to assess where financial assistance may be needed, we computed various items of expenditure. Inpatient hospital charges and the services of attending physicians are shown separately here to permit comparison with national data. However, for economy in presentation in other tables, physicians' services for inpatients are included as part of the total cost of hospitalization.

In our study, fees from attending physicians were 8% of the average total inpatient expenditures for individuals with autism and 15% of the average total inpatient expenditures for individuals with severe mental retardation. Patients with physical impairments generate a more intense medical effort shifting a greater proportion of the total inhospital expenditures toward doctor payments. Physician charges were 23% of the mean inpatient expenditures for individuals with mental retardation and severe physical impairments.

One of the interesting comparisons is to contrast medical expenditures for offspring cared for by their families to expenditures for those who lived in intermediate care facilities, group homes, or foster care. Table 5.6 compares health expenditures for individuals with autism living with their families against those living in residential care settings.

TABLE 5.5

Average Annual Expenses for Specific Health Services: Young Adults Age 18-24

SERVICE	AUTISM $N=63$	SEVERE MENTAL RETARDATION $N=91$
Hospital	$1,087 0-2,546	$1,654 23-2,224
Physicians during hospital stays	88 0-300	170 0-309
Physicians in private practice	158 30-162	317 31-744
Outpatient	101 0-177	184 50-438
Dentists	60 16-78	36 16-80
Allied health professionals	114 0-280	126 0-237
Drugs	159 0-274	228 0-346
Equipment	6 0-15	176 7-80
Supplies	10 0-33	248 0-770
Total	$1,783 196-3,427	$3,139 542-4,607

Note. The ranges show the average expenditures at the next to lowest and next to highest sites.

TABLE 5.6

Autism: Average Expenditures by Living Arrangement

SERVICE	AGE UNDER 18		AGE 18-24	
	HOME $N=238$	AWAY $N=13$	HOME $N=46$	AWAY $N=11$
Total inpatient[a]	$400	$200	$650	$2,000
Physicians in private practice	150	150	100	350
Outpatient	150	50	100	100
Dentists	50	50	50	50
Allied health professionals	150	400	100	200
Total	$1,000	$1,000	$1,300	$2,800

Note. Results have been rounded for presentation. Column totals include payments for drugs, equipment, supplies, and ambulance services that are not shown separately.
[a] Includes attending physician charges.

We found virtually no difference in expenditures for those under age 18. However, for the older group, those in residential care had medical expenses two times greater than those who lived at home. Hospital expenses for the residential care group were around $2,000, as compared to $650 for older autistic children living at home.

A very different pattern was revealed when we compared young adults with severe retardation according to place of residence, as can be seen in Table 5.7.

TABLE 5.7

Severe and Profound Mental Retardation: Average Expenditures by Living Arrangement

SERVICE	AGE UNDER 18		AGE 18-24	
	HOME $N=196$	AWAY $N=39$	HOME $N=58$	AWAY $N=33$
Total inpatient[a]	$2,000	$1,500	$2,500	$500
Physicians in private practice	300	2,000	200	500
Outpatient	400	300	200	200
Dentists	25	25	50	50
Allied health professionals	400	50	150	100
Total	$4,000	$5,000	$4,000	$2,000

Note. Results have been rounded for presentation. Column totals include payments for drugs, equipment, supplies, and ambulance services that are not shown separately.
[a] Includes attending physician charges.

Adults living at home had more frequent hospitalizations. As a result their annual health expenses were more than two times higher than the bill for adults in placements. As with autism, for children total expenditures were roughly the same, regardless of place of residence.

Hospital expenditures for the average stay for children with developmental disabilities are remarkably similar to revenues required for the average stay in an urban hospital, but more than the typical child's stay. The 1985 mean revenue of $4,613 per discharge was compiled by the National Center for Health Services Research. It included all charges for all ages incurred on an inpatient basis, excluding separate billings for inhospital physician visits or services.

In our sample of 140 hospitalizations of individuals with severe retardation, the average expenditures across sites ranged from $1,000 to $6,000, with the national average at $4,300. A similarly broad range across sites held for the 36 hospitalizations of individuals with autism, and the average of $4,600 was similar, too.

Health care resources are unequally distributed, with relatively few people consuming a large proportion of the care. One way to demonstrate how a relatively small percentage of each developmental disability category consumes a disproportionate share of the resources is to examine average expenses for only actual users. In this way, we can see how many patients were actually involved in receiving each service as well as how much each service charged.

TABLE 5.8

Autism: Average Expenditures Among Persons Who Used the Service

SERVICE	AGE UNDER 18		AGE 18-24	
	EXPENSES	NO. WHO USED THE SERVICE	EXPENSES	NO. WHO USED THE SERVICE
Total inpatient[a]	$3,500	23	$8,500	9
Outpatient	300	110	200	28
Physicians in private practice	150	259	150	63
Dentists	150	112	100	35
Allied health professionals	1,000	33	300	22
Drugs	100	259	150	63
Equipment	20	259	< 10	63
Supplies	70	259	< 30	63

Note. Results have been rounded for presentation.
[a] Includes attending physician charges.

Basic information on the per person expense *only for individuals using the service* is contained in Tables 5.8 and 5.9. The average expenditures here may be contrasted with those presented in Tables 5.4 and 5.5, which are for all children and young adults regardless of whether or not they received services. For instance, expenses for therapies and services of allied health professionals averaged about $150 across all autistic children. By contrast, we see in Table 5.8 that over $1,000 was spent for each of the few autistic children who had services.

The great width of the range results from variation in the type and amount of services by the few users as well as systematic differences in charges by allied health professionals in different localities. Only 32 members of the autism sample received inpatient services. Table 5.9 shows, in contrast, that 82 children in the severe mental retardation sample were hospitalized during the year of the study.

Expected differences when comparing only the members of the two disability groups who receive each service are that the average expenditure for each child with severe retardation is higher than for each autistic child. The higher rate of comorbidity among severely retarded children and young adults would explain this finding. An unexpected finding, however, is that the expenditure per child is consistently lower for dental services.

TABLE 5.9

Severe and Profound Mental Retardation: Average Expenditures Among Persons Who Used the Service

	AGE UNDER 18		AGE 18-24	
SERVICE	EXPENSES	NO. WHO USED THE SERVICE	EXPENSES	NO. WHO USED THE SERVICE
Total inpatient[a]	$6,000	66	$8,000	16
Outpatient	600	159	400	36
Physicians in private practice	350	239	300	92
Dentists	70	84	90	39
Allied health professional	2,000	46	500	21
Drugs	200	239	225	92
Equipment	300	239	100	92
Supplies	350	239	200	92

Note. Results have been rounded for presentation.
[a] Includes attending physician charges.

TABLE 5.10

Severe and Profound Mental Retardation: Average Expenditures Among Those Who Used the Service, by Ability to Walk

	AVERAGE ANNUAL EXPENDITURES							
	AGE UNDER 18				AGE 18-24			
	CAN WALK	N	CANNOT WALK WELL	N	CAN WALK	N	CANNOT WALK WELL	N
Total inpatient[a]	$4,000	6	$6,000	49	$2,000	5	$11,000	10
Outpatient	250	24	550	110	400	14	350	22
Physicians in private practice	200	60	400	148	200	39	300	54
Dentists	100	25	50	56	120	20	50	19
Allied health professionals	500	3	2,000	38	350	10	600	11
Drugs	100	60	250	148	150	39	250	54
Equipment	50	60	400	148	20	39	150	54
Supplies	100	60	400	54	20	39	200	148

Note. Ability to walk half a mile as judged by the parents is the criterion here. Children under age 4 are excluded.
[a] Includes attending physician charges.

We have made an analysis within the retarded group, distinguishing individuals with physically handicapping conditions. A good predictor of annual expenditures was the ability to walk half a mile, an item also included in the 1987 National Medical Expenditure Survey. The higher expenses for physically handicapped children and young adults is due both to a higher proportion using services and to their receiving more expensive services.

Across all 153 individuals with mental retardation who could neither walk half a mile nor climb 10 stairs, the average expenditure on hospital stays was $2,900 because more than one-third of them were hospitalized. By contrast, only $400 per person was spent on inpatient care for those who could walk well, since only 11 of the 75 were hospitalized.

The higher charges to users of service is shown in Table 5.10. Hospitalized children who could walk well averaged $4,000 in hospital charges, compared to $6,000 for children with impaired ambulation. Higher spending for individuals with difficulty ambulating is also pronounced for equipment, supplies, drugs, and allied health professionals.

OTHER EXPENDITURES FOR
INDIVIDUALS LIVING AT HOME

Up to this point, we have discussed the standard items of health care expenditures. Unfortunately, the standard definition of health care seriously neglects a large array of expenditures that developmentally disabled children need *due to their developmental disabilities.*

Families have a variety of concerns and expenses due to the persisting needs of their children for care far beyond the ages when other children can independently perform the usual activities of daily living. Tables 5.11 and 5.12 show special expenses that families incur to enable their child to live at home.

Child care includes regular child care in the family home or at the home of a sitter, but does not include occasional sitters. Special programs include after school, day, and weekend programs, summer school and summer camp. Overnight respite includes the child going elsewhere or a caretaker coming to the home. The category of travel to medical appointments includes transportation expenses, meals and overnight lodging, as required, babysitting for siblings, and extraordinary telephone expenses. Damage expense includes only actual expenditures for replacements and repairs during the study period.

In computing the cost of home modifications, as in all other categories, we included only expenses incurred during the 12 months of study. A car modification, although rare, was the most expensive item, defined as the difference in price between the vehicle the family actually purchased (typically a van) and the car they would have purchased if their child had not been in a wheelchair.

For children with autism, the total personal care expense that averaged about $600 per child is comparable to the $1,000 for average health expenses, previously shown in Table 5.4. For children with severe retardation, the personal care bill of about $900 was substantially less than their health care bill of about $4,000. The families of children with autism have considerable expense for child care, programs, such as after school or special camps, and repair or replacement of damaged household furnishings. The families of

severely retarded children have special expenses for child care, home modification, and travel to medical appointments.

TABLE 5.11

Persons Living At Home: Average Expenditures for Other Required Services

	AUTISM		SEVERE MENTAL RETARDATION	
SERVICE	AGE UNDER 18 N=238	AGE 18-24 N=46	AGE UNDER 18 N=196	AGE 18-24 N=58
Child care	$250	$50	$400	$190
Special programs	200	200	75	25
Respite	<10	<10	<10	25
Travel for medical services	50	50	175	60
Home and car modifications and damage replacements	100	10	250	300
Total	$600	$320	$900	600

Note. Results are rounded for presentation.

TABLE 5.12

Average Expenditures for Other Required Services Among Those Who Used the Service

AVERAGE ANNUAL EXPENDITURES

	AUTISM				SEVERE MENTAL RETARDATION			
	UNDER 18 YEARS	N	18-24 YEARS	N	UNDER 18 YEARS	N	18-24 YEARS	N
Child care	$2,700	26	$2,000	3	$2,000	42	$2,000	6
Special programs	1,000	43	400	29	600	20	150	13
Respite	150	19	50	3	200	4	175	11
Travel for medical service	50	236	50	60	200	214	75	74
Home and car modification and replacement	400	69	100	9	1,000	54	1,700	17

Note. Results have been rounded for presentation.

In order to estimate total expenditures for care at home, we aggregated
all expenses for special programs, paid caregivers, and respite services. Unpaid

services from relatives and friends were excluded because they are not expenses. The efforts made by parents to adapt their home or automobile to their child's needs and expenses for repairing damages caused by the child were included.

CONCLUSIONS

Despite the current professional view of mental retardation and autism as primarily problems that require interventions by educational and vocational rehabilitation agencies, the medical and health-related expenses for these two conditions were considerable. As with many other populations, such as the elderly, we found that a small percentage of each group accounted for most of the expenditures. In addition, we found that residential placement does not end the need for medical interventions, particularly for children or adults with serious functional deficits and medical problems.

In the case of autism, care for physical needs is not the major determinant of the use of the health care system, and reliance on psychiatric hospitalization increases as the person ages. If we consider family and residential placement as the essential care units for this dependent population, each unit may still require long-term hospital support for individuals who cannot be maintained in either setting. While only 9 persons with autism over the age of 18 in our sample were hospitalized during the study period, because of lengthy stays their charges averaged twice that of the 23 younger autistic persons who were hospitalized that year.

These expenditures not withstanding, the charges for *nonmedical* services used by families to maintain either a child with severe retardation or an autistic child at home were modest. This finding deserves further investigation in a carefully designed representative study of all expenditures in residential and home care.

Chapter 6

Third Party Coverage and the Uninsured

Over the past 40 years, health care as a proportion of the American gross national product has risen from 4% to more than 11%. Simultaneously, the proportion of the total personal health care expenditures paid by private insurance has risen from 9% to 31% in 1980 and then remained at that plateau. The share paid by public sources also rose,from 22% in 1950 to 40% in 1975, and then stayed level.

Americans as a whole by 1988 were paying out-of-pocket for 24% of their personal health care bill (Waldo, Sonnefeld, McKusich, & Arnett, 1990). This burden of payments falls heavily among the 34 million Americans who lack health insurance and especially upon those who have serious chronic conditions.

The findings reported in this chapter can be organized into two broad categories: (a) the likelihood of health insurance for a child varies by age, parents' employment, and geographic region; (b) the possession of insurance coverage predicts more comprehensive care. A final brief section describes how recent trends have adversely affected children's insurance coverage, setting the stage for the following chapter on who pays for what.

THE BROAD PATTERNS OF
INSURANCE COVERAGE

Compared to the general population under age 24, individuals with autism or with severe or profound mental retardation are much better covered by public programs, as shown in Table 6.1.

The national data are initial published findings from the 1987 National Medical Expenditure Survey, which did not create a separate category for individuals with both private and public coverage, but in the future will provide a plentitude of comparative statistics.

About half the individuals with autism have private insurance alone and about one quarter have only public coverage. These proportions are roughly reversed for children and young adults with severe retardation. The table shows that the severely retarded children and young adults in our study are less well covered by private insurance than the average American young person, but that public programs prevent many from being uninsured.

TABLE 6.1

Health Insurance Coverage of the Sample Compared to National Averages

GROUP	N	NONE	PUBLIC	PRIVATE	BOTH
Autism	308	7% 0-18	26% 16-28	49% 47-59	19% 11-22
Severe mental retardation	326	4 0-9	43 27-47	25 13-39	28 17-36
U.S. 0-24 years	–	20.2	11.2	68.2	–[a]

Note. Below each mean percentage is the range, representing the next to lowest and next to highest site means. U.S. 1987 data are from *A Profile of Uninsured Americans*, 1989, National Center for Health Services Research, Rockville, MD: Public Health Service.

[a]The source cited did not create a separate category for those with public and private coverage; these individuals are included in the "private" category.

The percentages on young people with developmental disabilities are consistent with all the data presented in this monograph, weighted to represent metropolitan America. The ranges showing low and high site averages are wide because sites differ greatly in providing private and public health coverage.

INADEQUACY OF PRIVATE
HEALTH INSURANCE COVERAGE

The historical fact that health insurance began in America as a fringe benefit from employers explains the tremendous variation in coverage and deficiencies in coverage by industry or region. At the same time these patterns developed, national health expenditures rose from $41 billion in 1965 to $458 billion in 1986, from 6% of the GNP to 11%, making cost containment an important issue.

Furthermore, in order to fully appreciate the dynamics of insurance coverage, another trend must enter the equation. The decline of "smokestack" industries is significant because industrial unions have sought and obtained fringe benefits. The percentage of the nonagricultural labor force in unions has dropped from 29% in 1964 to 22% today, accounting for employers' cutting back on health benefits. Businesses today are more likely to hire part-time employees and women whose husbands are covered by other plans. Families with chronically disabled children are caught in these national trends, as are all families.

It is common in the United States for both parents to be in the work force. Table 6.2 shows for the study population how the parents' employment status related to the coverage of children and young adults living at home. When both parents had full-time employment, private health insurance covered almost 100% of the children with autism and almost 90% of the children with severe retardation. However, in families where only one parent was working full-time, the proportions for both disabilities dropped by approximately 15 percentage points. There is even more cause for concern for the roughly one fifth of the children whose parents had only part-time employment; roughly one third of these children have private coverage. About 20% had private insurance when no parent was employed.

TABLE 6.2

Private Health Insurance Coverage Among Individuals Living at Home

| | PERCENTAGE COVERED | |
CHARACTERISTIC	AUTISM N=284	SEVERE MENTAL RETARDATION N=254
Parents' work status		
2 full-time	98%	90%
1 full-time	80	75
Part-time or unemployed	20	25
Age		
Under 18 years	70	60
18-24 years	50	40
Race		
White	70	60
Black	50	30

Note. Results are rounded for presentation.

Does the age of the disabled person make a difference? About 70% of children with autism had private insurance, but only about 50% of young adults. A similar drop occurs between childhood and adulthood for people with severe mental retardation, from about 60% to about 40%.

This phenomenon can be explained by referring to the American population as a whole. Young adults are the age group least covered by health insurance. In 1987, 29% of 19 to 24-year-olds had neither public nor private insurance, compared to 17% of children and 16% of 24 to 54-year-olds who are at the national average (National Center for Health Services Research, 1987).

Employment as the basis of private insurance is the key explanation, because young adults outgrow eligibility for their parents' policies but tend to take jobs where the employer does not provide health insurance, such as in the fast food industry. Severely retarded and autistic young adults are rarely covered by their parents' policies because they outgrow eligibility at age 18, or at 21 if they continue their enrollment in special education.

The type of employment strongly influences the degree of continuity of private insurance coverage, with lows of 73% of year-round coverage for laborers and 74% for service workers, as of 1977, while professionals are covered nearly 100%.

The consequences of minority group members' disproportionate employment in unskilled positions shows up in our data. We found that less than one third of all severely retarded black children and young adults were covered by private health insurance, half the rate for whites, as shown in Table 6.2. The difference for black children compared to white children holds even when taking into account whether or not a parent was working full time and whether or not family income was above $15,000.

Among those with autism, at least, the racial disparity was not as pronounced. For Americans as a whole, strong regional disparities persist in insurance coverage. The 1984 measurement by the Current Population Survey found 12% uninsured in the East and in the North, but 18% in the South and in the West. Our sample sites had more extreme differences. No disabled child or young adult was uninsured in the Detroit metropolitan area sample of 181, nor was anyone uninsured with autism who lived in the Birmingham area nor anyone with severe mental retardation living in the New York metropolitan area. However, 20% of the Dallas children with autism and 10% of the Fresno children with severe mental retardation had no insurance.

PUBLIC HEALTH INSURANCE COVERAGE

Medicaid is the most common public program serving these children with autism and severe mental retardation. Next in coverage is the Title V program, Services for Children with Special Health Needs, formerly known as Crippled Children's Services. Among the scattering of state and local programs, the one that is available to all children with these disabilities is the Michigan family supplement of $225 per month, for the parents to use as they choose.

Racial disparity in private insurance is compensated for by public coverage. For both white and black families, Medicaid and other public programs bring coverage to over 90% for children with autism and to over 95% for children with severe mental retardation. In general, the families that are economically the neediest are best served by public programs. Families with annual incomes under $15,000 are about three times as likely to have public coverage as families with higher incomes, and single mothers are about twice as likely to have public coverage for their children as married couples.

Walter, a four-year-old with Down syndrome and a congenital heart defect, provides an example of the complexity of who pays for medical services. Walter's father is self-employed and had carried health care insurance for his wife and two sons. After Walter's birth, the prohibitive expense for a policy to cover him sent the family to look to SSI as a route to Medicaid coverage. In Walter's first year of life the family's difficult financial circumstances made them eligible for $367 per month in SSI payments and Medicaid coverage for the infant. When the father's income increased, the family was able to hold on to $11 per month in SSI income and, despite the SSI demand that the family refund $10,000 in overpayment, to maintain Walter's Medicaid coverage.

After the study period, Walter had open heart surgery for a total expenditure of $150,000, but the family did not know for months whether or not Medicaid would cover the costs.

The great divide between 17 and 18 that separates young adults from their parents' private insurance is compensated for by Medicaid. Unemployment as the basis for Medicaid eligibility insurance works to the advantage of these disabled young adults. Severely mentally retarded 18-year-olds become categorically eligible for Social Security Insurance because they are incapable of gainful employment. In 1985, autistic adults, as well, became categorically eligible for SSI due to a change in the regulations. The strong role of public coverage for the young adult leaves few uninsured.

A surprising finding is that the levels of physical impairment among individuals covered by Medicaid were no higher than among those not covered. Children who are multiply impaired have greater need for Medicaid because of their higher use of medical services. Marked inequities exist in public coverage by place of residence. Medicaid and Title V programs are so extensive in the Detroit, Birmingham, and Fresno areas that they covered about 70% of both disability groups. By contrast, only about 40% had public coverage in Dallas and only 50% in Jacksonville, in two southern states with restrictive eligibility rules for Medicaid.

TABLE 6.3

Percentage Insurance Coverage for Children Under Age 18 in the Study Compared to All U.S. Children at the Four Levels of Limitation of Activity

| | U.S. POPULATION | | | | | |
INSURANCE COVERAGE	WITHOUT LIMITS	LA-3	LA-2	LA-1	AUTISM	SEVERE MENTAL RETARDATION
U.S. population in '000s	59,507	922	1,916	224	25	75
Private	76%	80%	67%	55%	71%	58%
Medicaid	10	11	20	28	28	48
Other public	<1	1	2	5	10	28
None	15	11	14	18	7	4
Total	101%	103%	103%	106%	116%	138%
N	5,996	75	156	18	251	235

Note. U.S. data in columns 1 to 4 are from the 1980 NMCUES which had a sample of 6,245 children (Kasper, 1986). The data in columns 5 and 6 are from this study.

THE UNINSURED

One third of the nation's uninsured population are children, more than 12 million. Table 6.3 is a second way to put our findings in national perspective against the 1980 NMCUES data, shown in the first four columns of the table. Because the 1987 NMES data describing insurance coverage for children at different activity levels are not yet available, the 1980 data can be adjusted to 1986 by noting that private insurance for children as a whole had dropped 3 percentage points during those years.

This table shows children divided according to their degree of limitation of activity. There were almost 60 million children without limits in activity. The most limited in activity are in the LA-1 category used by the National Center for Health Statistics, defined as those unable to attend school. The children in our samples may be compared to these 224,000 children and to the almost 2 million children in LA-2, those who attend or need to attend special classes because of an impairment or health problem.

The number of autistic children in the United States is estimated at about 25,000 by applying Wing's estimation of prevalence at between .4 and .5 per 1,000 (Wing & Gould, 1979). The number of children with severe and profound mental retardation is estimated at about 75,000, based on a prevalence of about 1.2 per 1,000.

Of children who had no limitation of activity, 76% were covered by private insurance, 10% by Medicaid, and 15% were uninsured in 1980. The coverage by each major type of health insurance is shown separately, thus making the total coverage add to over 100%. Note that the proportion of children with multiple insurance coverage increases as the severity of disability increases. Especially noteworthy is the increase in Medicaid coverage as limitation of activity increases. The conclusion is that children with serious developmental disabilities are more likely to have public coverage and more likely to have multiple coverage than the typical child with limited activity.

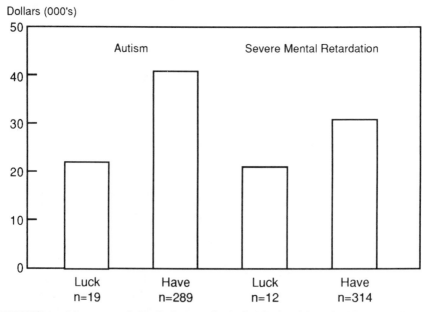

FIGURE 6.1: Mean annual family income for individuals with and without any health insurance.

Figure 6.1 begins to answer the question of who are the uninsured among the children with autism and severe retardation.

They are the poorer. For uninsured children and young adults in both disability categories, the mean family income is about $20,000. The mean income of those with public or private insurance is about $40,000 for those with autism and about $30,000 for those with severe mental retardation.

Discontinuity of insurance coverage for children is a serious problem when parents change jobs and move in and out of eligibility for Medicaid. The NMCUES survey sampled families at four points during a year and found 7% without insurance during the whole year and 14% insured for only part of a year. Our finding of roughly 5% lacking insurance for part of the year appears to be an underestimate because we had to rely on parents' recall at the time of the interview to cover the preceding twelve months, a less certain method than the NMCUES repeated interviews at three month intervals. However, a reason to believe that these developmentally disabled individuals have more continuity of coverage than the average child and young adult is that mental deficiency triggers categorical eligibility for permanent Medicaid coverage. Other youngsters covered by Medicaid through Aid to Families with Dependent Children or by private plans lose and gain insurance as the parents change employment status.

Parents of children with serious chronic conditions experience two unresolved problems in health insurance coverage: refusals and exclusions. The proportion of parents who replied "Yes" to the question, "Have you or (CHILD'S FATHER/MOTHER) ever been refused health insurance for (CHILD) or limited in the kind of health insurance you could buy because of (CHILD'S) condition?" was almost 20% for children with severe retardation and about 10% for children with autism.

Refusals and limitations were more frequently experienced by parents living in Dallas and Jacksonville than in the North and East, and single-parent families experienced refusals at slightly higher rates than two-parent families. The mean family income of those refused in both disability groups was about $25,000. By contrast, the mean income for families who never experienced a refusal was $5,000 higher for children with severe mental retardation and $10,000 higher for children with autism.

Underinsurance is a more widespread problem than total lack of coverage. In both disability categories, about 15% of the parents answered "yes" to the question, "Does the insurance which covers the family specifically exclude coverage for any of (CHILD'S) care?" Families experienced exclusions in all sites, and equally between holders of Blue Cross policies and commercial insurers, and even among the 8% of families enrolled in HMOs. A pioneering study of HMOs serving children in three disability categories, developmental delay, leukemia, and cystic fibrosis (Karlson, Sumi, & Braucht, 1990), found that HMOs were like fee-for-service insurance in restricting coverage of services for habilitation and personal care.

The metaphor of the patchwork quilt illustrates health insurance coverage for American children with developmental disabilities. Children under age 18 with autism provide a characteristic example of the fragmentation. About one half are covered by a single private insurance policy. Approximately one sixth are covered by two private policies. About one sixth are covered by Medicaid alone. About 5% have multiple coverage of Medicaid plus private insurance, and another 5% have additional coverage from programs for Children with Special Health Needs. However, roughly 7% have no coverage at all.

HEALTH CARE CONSEQUENCES
OF LACK OF INSURANCE

Children lacking health insurance are likely to have fewer physician visits, as reported in Tables 4.5 and 4.6 of the chapter on utilization. About one quarter of the autistic children lacking insurance had no physician visits, as did about 15% of the children with severe retardation.

An even larger proportion of uninsured children failed to see a physician annually, as reported in Butler et al. (1987), a study of children in special education in five sites. These investigators found that in children who had a high prevalence condition: speech impairment, learning disabilities, attention deficits, and emotional and behavioral problems, 62% of insured children had physician visits in the previous 12 months compared to 39% of the uninsured. The proportions were similar, 78% to 53%, for children with low prevalence conditions: mental retardation, hearing or vision impairments, neuromuscular, physical or orthopedic problems, and chronic illness.

In our study we asked the standard questions, "Is there a particular clinic, health center, doctor's office, or other place that you usually go if (CHILD) is *sick* or you need advice about (his/her) *general* health?" and "Is there a particular doctor that (CHILD) sees?" In addition we asked, "Is there a place you *usually* take (CHILD) for advice or treatment concerning his/her (DISABILITY)?"

If parents told us they got advice on the disability from their child's primary physician, the child was included in this discussion as having a source of specialty care. Table 6.3 shows that possession of insurance coverage predicts having a regular physician and a source of disability care. In the autistic sample, only about three quarters of the children and young adults without insurance had a regular physician. If individuals had public insurance alone, the proportion became about 75%, and if they had private insurance alone or in combination, the proportion was about 90%. Hardly any of the uninsured had a source of disability care, and among the insured less than half did. Among individuals with severe retardation, both of these patterns are repeated. A larger proportion of the severely retarded sample, at each level of insurance coverage, had a regular source of disability care.

TABLE 6.4

Insurance Coverage Predicts Having Usual Sources of Care for Children and Young Adults

	% HAVING CARE BY INSURANCE COVERAGE		
GROUP INSURANCE	NONE	PUBLIC ONLY	PRIVATE AND PUBLIC
Autism			
Regular physician	55%	75%	90%
Regular disability care	15%	25%	30%
N	19	85	204
Severe mental retardation			
Regular physician	40%	75%	90%
Regular disability care	25%	40%	50%
N	12	133	181

Note. Included in the third column are those with private insurance alone. See Table 6.1 for the proportions. Figures are rounded for presentation.

THE UPWARD TREND AND RECENT PLATEAU IN HEALTH INSURANCE COVERAGE

Many employees recently have had to pay more deductibles and copayments related to their medical and hospital insurance claims. Cost shifting not only is considered necessary by employers to hold down their fringe benefit expenses, but also is seen as making covered employees more cost conscious. Since 1980, third party payments have stood still as a proportion of health care expenditures with the consequence that people are paying more out-of-pocket.

Let us look at some details of recent trends in private health insurance for those who are best insured, people working full time for large and medium sized firms. Using data from the Bureau of Labor Statistics, Figure 6.2 shows that $100 had been the standard deductible, but after 1982 the percentage of plan participants who had to pay deductibles of $150 or more shot up from 7% to 36%.

Employers' cost containment efforts work against coverage for dependent children in two ways: a requirement that the employee pay a premium and the size of the premium. Among employees who chose single coverage, firms pay the entire premium for 54%. However, among employees choosing family coverage, the firms pay the premium for only 35%. In plans where the employee contributes a monthly premium, Figure 6.3 shows that the average amount for single coverage has risen little since 1979, from $10 to only $13 per month, while premiums for family coverage have grown from $28 to $41 per month.

Percent

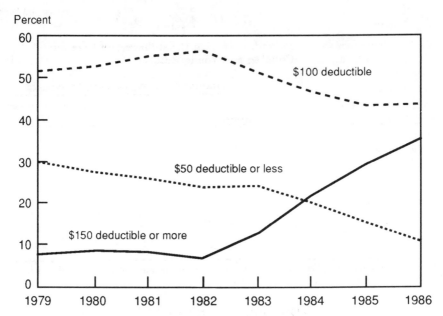

FIGURE 6.2: Trends in deductibles, reprinted from *Employee benefits in medium and large firms, 1986* (Bulletin 2281), p.29, by the Bureau of Labor Statistics, 1987. Washington, DC: U.S. Government Printing Office.

Monthly Contribution (dollars)

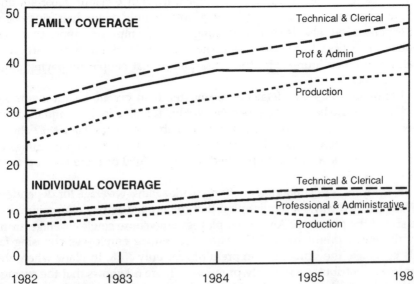

FIGURE 6.3: Employee contributions for health care benefits, reprinted from *Employee benefits in medium and large firms, 1986* (Bulletin 2281), p.32, by the Bureau of Labor Statistics, 1987. Washington, DC: U.S. Government Printing Office.

Data from the Census Bureau in Table 6.5 show the consequences for children. In 1980, children were five percentage points behind adults in their coverage by group health insurance, 64% to 69%. By 1985, children had fallen slightly more than six percentage points behind adults. Turning to Medicaid in Table 6.6, we see that the Current Population Surveys show that the percentage of children covered held generally steady between 1980 and 1985.

That is, the problem steadily persisted through 1985; half of the nation's children in poverty were not covered by Medicaid. Congressional legislation in the Budget Reconciliation Acts has taken a series of steps to expand Medicaid coverage, to be discussed in chapter 10.

The next chapter will show exactly how the families of the children in our study are affected by these stagnant and adverse trends.

TABLE 6.5

Percent with Group Health Insurance

| YEAR | CHILDREN UNDER 18 YEARS | | ADULTS 18-64 YEARS | |
	OLD SERIES	NEW SERIES	OLD SERIES	NEW SERIES*
1980	63.9%		68.8%	
1981	63.1		68.8	
1982	61.9		66.5	
1983	60.8		65.5	
1984	60.7		64.9	
1985	60.6		66.7	
1986	61.1		67.7	
1987	59.9	64.1%	66.7	67.2%
1988		63.9		67.0

Note. The source is unpublished census data, Income Statistics, Current Population Surveys. The new series is based on an improved questionnaire that asks directly about the insurance coverage of every member of the household.

TABLE 6.6

Medicaid Coverage of American Children

YEAR	TOTAL CHILDREN IN '000s	% MEDICAID	CHILDREN IN POVERTY IN '000s	% POOR IN MEDICAID
1980	63,684	12%	11,269	46%
1981	63,243	13	12,234	46
1982	62,891	13	13,373	57
1983	62,691	13	13,560	48
1984	62,689	13	13,142	49
1985	62,953	13	12,696	51
1986	63,084	13	12,501	52
1987	63,438	14	12,697	53

Note. The source is unpublished census data, Income Statistics, Current Population Surveys.

Chapter 7

The Financing of Services

The complex pattern of insurance coverage described in the previous chapter gives rise to complex funding arrangements. A careful description of the funding streams serves two purposes. First, a policy perspective should be built on knowledge of how existing financing mechanisms are working. The policy recommendations presented in the concluding chapter draw directly on the descriptions presented here. Second, the family perspective continues the theme of hardship caused by the very complexity of the financial arrangements and lays the basis for the next chapter on out-of-pocket payments.

Health care services are grouped into six categories for this analysis. Inpatient hospital services and physician services during the hospital stay are shown together as total inpatient expenditures. Outpatient hospital services include clinics, emergency rooms, and a sprinkling of free-standing emergency centers. The physician category is composed of physicians in group and solo practice. The dental category encompasses all types of ambulatory dentistry including orthodontics, but excludes overnight hospitalization for dental work. Drugs include only prescription medication. Supplies include bandages, diapers, and other disposable items required because of the individual's condition.

Direct medical expenditures for therapy services delivered in private practice and for equipment have been described in chapter 5, but are excluded here due to methodological problems in making accurate estimations. We estimate that these omitted expenses constitute less than 1% of the total expenditures for both children with autism and those with severe and profound mental retardation.

POLICY FOCUS

Autism

Given that the United States has a basic private insurance system with overlays of public insurance and charitable programs, it is surprising to learn that private insurance pays only about 22% of the health care bill of autistic children under age 18, as shown in Table 7.1. Recall that about 70% of these children are covered by their parents' insurance. For American children as a whole, private insurance covers a similar proportion, 75%. For every type of service except hospitalization, the parents of a child with autism are paying more than the total from private insurance.

Medicaid and the family each support one third of the health care expenditures of autistic children. Over 10% of the charges are absorbed by the providers. The category "free from the provider" has three components: the shortfall of Medicaid reimbursement compared to the provider charges; free services; and the shortfall of private insurance payments where the family did not pay the balance.

Acceptance of Medicaid reimbursements that are well below standard charges is the largest component of the "free from provider category." Medicaid requires that providers accept their payments as reimbursement in full, and rates for the same procedures vary markedly across states. After Medicaid shortfalls, free services are the next largest means by which providers subsidize care, and the least common way is through acceptance of private insurance payment as payment in full.

The picture changes when the autistic child reaches age 18, showing a substantial rise in Medicaid payments from about one third to about half of the health care bills. This increase is accounted for primarily by the rise in the proportion of individuals who obtain Medicaid coverage through their SSI eligibility, an increase from one fifth to three quarters. The amount subsidized by the provider through acceptance of low Medicaid rates is larger than the drop in the amount paid by private insurance, benefiting the family purse. All together, the family's burden drops from one third to about one tenth.

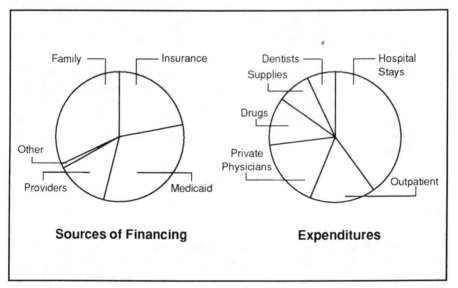

FIGURE 7.1: Sources of financing and health care expenditures for children with autism (under age 18)

TABLE 7.1

Autism: Health Care Financing for Children

PAYERS	HOSPITAL STAYS[a]	MDs IN PRIVATE PRACTICE	OUT-PATIENT	DENTISTS	DRUGS	SUPPLIES	TOTAL
		AVERAGE PAYMENT (N=259, UNDER AGE 18)					
Family	$12	$60	$52	$47	$38	$68	$278
	0-14	37-71	24-71	28-63	15-33	36-112	224-328
Insurance	72	33	45	6	32	0	188
	0-116	11-39	11-81	0-11	13-37		81-277
Medicaid	222	18	13	3	28	0	285
	0-530	7-29	6-22	0-3	0-21		65-565
CSHN[b]	4	0.2	0.8	0.04	0.2	0.4	5
	0-0	0-0	0-0	0-0	0-0	0-0	0-0
Free from provider	41	38	25	6	4	.2	114
	0-13	20-43	14-41	.2-8	2-5	0-0	48-103
Other sources	0	3	0.4	2	0.4	0	5
	.5-5	0-0	0-0	0-0	0-11		
Total	$351	$152	$136	$64	$103	$69	$875
No. who used the service	23	218	110	117	259	259	259

[a]Includes attending physician charges.
[b]Title V programs for Children with Special Health Needs.

Table 7.1 provides details on the categories of direct medical expenditures. The dollars spent on the average autistic child are shown for each major type of service and for each major source of payment, and the totals in the bottom row and last column are the basis of the pie charts in Figure 7.1. As in previous chapters, we give both the rounded average from the entire sample and, in selected tables, the range in averages across sites as a means of estimating the amount of confidence to place in the overall average.

For children, we see hospitalizations paid for heavily by Medicaid, relieving the families of all but about 5% of the burden. There are strong consistencies across the other types of service with the family serving as the largest payer, typically paying about one third while private insurance and providers about equally cover the rest. Dentistry is the glaring exception. Families paid over 70% of the bill and roughly 10% was free from the provider. We conclude that the pronounced underutilization of dental services, is explained not only by the difficulty of treating an uncooperative child, but also by the lack of third party payments.

The financing of services provided under Title V totaled less than 1% of the overall expenditure on children with autism because only 3% of these children in the sample had Title V coverage, but, as we will see shortly, this coverage was crucial to the few reached. Financing by a miscellany of other payers also totaled less than 1%.

A similar picture for young adults with autism emerges from Table 7.2. The dollar amount spent on each type of service was roughly the same as for children, except that hospital expenditures were at least twice as high. The lack of dental coverage continued into adulthood, slightly abated as Medicaid payments rose from 5% to 25%, cutting parental obligation from over 70% to 50% of the dental bill. The consistent shift is that Medicaid becomes the largest payer for every service, except dental care and medical supplies.

Because Medicaid is a parsimonious payer, the proportion contributed by the provider goes up for each type of service as the proportion of the bill paid by Medicaid goes up. A specific example is the roughly $150 average expenditure for services from physicians in private practice, shown in Table 7.1. Medicaid directly paid 12% of the total dollars (in the neighborhood of $12 per child with autism, including those not served). However,if physicians had received payment for the full amount they billed Medicaid, about $14 more per child with autism, would have been added to Medicaid payments and subtracted from the category "free from the provider."

For young adults, Table 7.2 shows that Medicaid increased to one third of the payment to physicians and to half the total expenditure. The shortfall in reimbursement to physicians and hospitals and the contribution of free services increased to one third of the total payment picture. The substantial expansion of Medicaid coverage as the children become adults reduces the amount that the family pays for each type of medical service, equipment, and supplies.

TABLE 7.2

Autism: Health Care Financing for Young Adults

PAYERS	AVERAGE PAYMENT (N=63, AGE 18-24)						
	HOSPITAL STAYS[a]	MDs IN PRIVATE PRACTICE	OUT-PATIENT	DENTISTS	DRUGS	SUPPLIES	TOTAL
Family	$25	$15	$10	$30	$40	$10	$130
Insurance	50	40	10	5	15	0	120
Medicaid	650	50	40	15	70	5	830
CSHN[b]	0	0	0	0	0	0	0
Free from provider	475	50	40	10	20	5	600
Other sources	0	0	0	0	0	0	0
Total	$1,200	$155	$100	$60	$145	$20	$1,680
No. who used the service	10	53	28	39	63	63	63

Note. Results have been rounded for presentation.
[a]Includes attending physician charges.
[b]Title V program for Children with Special Health Needs.

Just 8 children are served by Title V programs out of the sample of 251 children with autism. The $400 average total expenditure for these eight children is half the average for all autistic children, and the pattern is very different. The $170 CSHN average contribution per child finances more of the services than private insurance, Medicaid, and the family combined. Free services from the providers, averaging $120, make up the balance.

Severe and Profound Mental Retardation

In turning to children with severe and profound retardation, we should bear in mind that their average health care bill is about four times as high as the bill for children with autism. Figure 7.2 shows that the sharing of the payments was similar to autism, with about half of the charges paid by Medicaid and private insurance and with families' and providers' contributions taking care of the rest. Almost one quarter of the total came from providers accepting reduced payments, about 3% is from Title V, and about 4% from other public and private programs. Although, the families of children with severe retardation on average paid only 16% of the health care bill, that expense was double the $300 average that parents of autistic children paid.

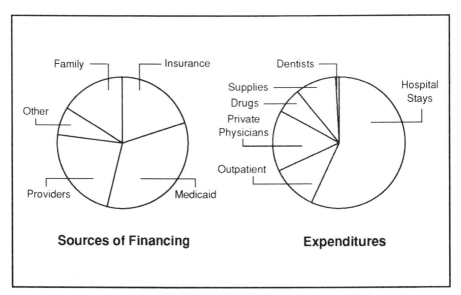

FIGURE 7.2: Sources of financing and health care expenditures for children with severe or profound mental retardation (under age 18)

In Table 7.3 we see that the largest average expense of families and of every payer was hospital stays. Families paid about one tenth of the hospital bills, Medicaid covered about one third, and private insurance and contributions from the provider each totaled about one quarter. For physicians in private practice, Medicaid was by far the largest payer, with the result that their "contributions" in accepting Medicaid fees rather than their standard fees resulted in the physicians contributing more in free and reduced-price services than they received in payment from private insurance and families.

For visits to hospital outpatient departments, the largest source of financing was the hospital contribution. In dentistry, the family and the dentists shared the financing. For prescription drugs, Medicaid, private insurance, and the family shared the cost. By contrast, medical and other supplies, such as diapers, that are necessitated by the child's condition fell heavily upon families. The total expenditure for supplies was about as large as the expense for outpatient treatment and twice the expense for drugs.

TABLE 7.3

Severe and Profound Retardation: Health Care Financing for Children

PAYERS	AVERAGE PAYMENT (N=237, UNDER AGE 18)						
	HOSPITAL STAYS[a]	MDs IN PRIVATE PRACTICE	OUT-PATIENT	DENTISTS	DRUGS	SUPPLIES	TOTAL
Family	$231	$63	$82	$9	$46	$192	$623
	.5-306	14-114	39-114	1-20	23-77	152-291	327-928
Insurance	516	38	76	2	64	57	753
	124-949	13-66	73-105	0-4	18-124	0-46	239-1206
Medicaid	730	298	83	5	74	91	1,281
	0-1012	0-105	32-113	0-6	0-95	0-99	42-2173
CSHN[b]	79	2	6	.4	2	19	108
	0-191	0-.4	0-10	0-0	0-0	0-.5	0-201
Free from provider	455	163	173	11	21	41	864
	.8-410	60-129	25-201	.03-15	8-24	14-76	262-796
Other sources	161	.4	3	0	.4	0	165
	0-231	0-0	0-6		0-0		0-231
Total	$2,172	$564	$423	$27	$207	$400	$3,793
No. who used the service	66	202	159	96	239	239	239

[a]Includes attending physician charges.
[b]Title V programs for Children with Special Health Needs.

State programs of Services for Children with Special Health Needs (CSHN) cover few children with autism and 58 children with severe retardation out of the 239 in the sample. Given the diversity of CSHN programs across the eight states in the sample, we believe that a reasonable generalization is that in urban and suburban America as a whole, one quarter of all children with severe or profound retardation are served by Title V programs.

TABLE 7.4

Severe and Profound Retardation: Health Care Financing for Children in Programs for Children with Special Health Needs

PAYERS	HOSPITAL STAYS[a]	MDs IN PRIVATE PRACTICE	OUT-PATIENT	DENTISTS	DRUGS	SUPPLIES	TOTAL
		AVERAGE PAYMENT (N=54, UNDER AGE 18)					
Family	$0	$0	$0	$1	$20	$200	$230
Insurance	1,900	20	150	1	25	200	2,300
Medicaid	2,000	200	90	1	70	175	2,500
CSHN[b]	330	10	25	2	10	75	450
Free from provider	0	200	350	15	25	60	650
Other sources	160	2	4	0	2	0	170
Total	$4,400	$450	$600	$20	$165	$700	$6,300
No. who used the service	21	49	46	26	42	43	54

Note. Due to rounding, rows and columns do not sum to totals.
[a]Includes attending physician charges.
[b]Title V programs for Children with Special Health Needs.

Table 7.4 shows that for the 54 children where we have data on CSHN assistance, their average expenses were $2,500 higher than those of the typical severely retarded child. These children had a higher rate of hospitalization, the major factor explaining higher expenses. Almost all had orthopedic disabilities, which in most states is a categoric criterion for eligibility for CSHN programs. As with the other children, private insurance and Medicaid picked up the largest portions of hospital bills and of the total bill.

The average CSHN payment was about $450, reducing the family's share to about $230, roughly $400 less than the average family with a child who has severe mental retardation. These families are fully protected against paying out-of-pocket for hospital and physician bills. If they lacked Title V coverage, their levels of financial obligation would be like the typical family with a severely retarded child.

Table 7.5 shows that after a child with severe retardation reaches 18, the family's dollar outlay and share of total payments go down. The Medicaid share goes up, particularly for drugs and supplies, while the private insurance share goes down for most goods and services and especially for physician services. By happenstance, in this particular sample of 92 young adults, some expensive hospital stays were covered by private insurance, which pushed the insurance share artificially high. Insurance expenditures for all other services had averaged about $235 for children but only $50 for young adults.

TABLE 7.5

Severe and Profound Retardation: Health Care Financing for Young Adults

		AVERAGE PAYMENT (N=92, AGE 18-24)					
PAYERS	HOSPITAL STAYS[a]	MDs IN PRIVATE PRACTICE	OUT-PATIENT	DENTISTS	DRUGS	SUPPLIES	TOTAL
Family	$0	$10	$5	$15	$20	$75	$125
Insurance	850	10	25	5	10	0	$900
Medicaid	500	140	60	10	150	100	$960
CSHN[b]	0	0	0	0	0	0	0
Free from provider	200	100	90	10	25	75	$500
Other sources	15	0	1	0	0	0	$15
Total	$1,565	$260	$180	$40	$205	$250	$2,500
No. who used the service	16	74	36	41	92	92	92

Note. Results have been rounded for presentation.
[a]Includes attending physician charges.
[b]Title V programs for Children with Special Health Needs.

FAMILY PERSPECTIVE

Financing health care is complex both from a system perspective and from a family perspective. Parents have difficulty finding appropriate providers and finding sources of payment for their services. Lacking a case manager, parents can use a workbook such as the one in the Georgetown University series to take charge of their child's health care (Kaufman & Lichtenstein, 1986). However, families with case management were more likely to have two private insurance policies, be enrolled in the CSHN program, carry a small burden of medical debt, and believe that medical services had helped to improve their child's life. Looking at severely retarded children in two-parent families, which generally have more resources than single parent families, we see that case management makes a difference.

Two boys with profound retardation from the Detroit area provide a contrast in how some families have large out-of-pocket expenses and others find resources to meet their child's medical needs. Craig, age 10, was born three weeks prematurely with microcephaly, quadriplegia, and orthopedic deformities. He also has vision problems, a seizure disorder, and chronic asthma. He is unable to take care of any of his daily functions, including feeding himself. Craig neither talks nor seeks the company of other people.

During the year of the study he had seven visits to a physician. A pediatrician on the verge of retirement is his primary physician. She hospitalized him once during the year for orthopedic problems, but he sees no specialist as a usual source of care. His mother holds no paid employment because she cares for Craig and three younger brothers, none of whom are disabled. His two grandmothers come over regularly for a few hours a week to help care for him. The $28,000 in wages that his father earns as a carpenter are insufficient to cover Craig's annual expenses for health care, which totaled $4,821. The top of Table 7.6 shows the distribution of expenses and payment sources for Craig.

TABLE 7.6

Comparison of Financing for Two Boys with Quadriplegia

PAYERS	HOSPITAL STAYS[a]	MDs IN PRIVATE PRACTICE	OUT-PATIENT	DENTISTS	DRUGS	SUPPLIES	TOTAL
	AVERAGE PAYMENT (N=92, AGE 18-24)						
Craig, Age 10							
Family	0	0	0	0	0	0	0
Insurance	$4,232	0	$106	0	0	0	$4,338
CSHN[b]	0	46	0	0	253	0	299
Free from provider	0	184	0	0	0	0	184
Total	$4,232	$230	$106	0	$253	0	$4,821
Joseph, Age 4							
Family	$50	$35	$741	0	$108	$240	$1,174
Insurance	2,965	0	28	0	0	0	2,993
CSHN[b]	0	0	0	0	0	0	0
Free from provider	0	0	0	0	0	0	0
Total	$3,015	$35	$769	0	$108	$240	$4,167

[a]Includes attending physician charges.
[b]Title V programs for Children with Special Health Needs.

Craig is fortunate in having both case management and services from the Michigan program of Services for Children with Special Health Needs. A variety of sources have removed the need for the family to pay anything out-of-pocket for Craig's direct medical expenses. The financing and services are orchestrated by the Detroit Institute for Children, which has provided a case manager for Craig since his birth. Services for Children with Special Health Needs picks up precisely those expenses that the insurance policy does not cover, prescription drugs and a physician's bill. The family has the advantage of living in Michigan, where the Family Support Subsidy Program for developmentally disabled children provides $225 a month for the family's discretionary spending.

Joseph, now age four, is similarly disabled: quadriplegia, orthopedic deformities, a seizure disorder, and vision problems. Like Craig, Joseph is unable to take care of his bodily needs, nor does he speak or seek sociability. He has a pediatrician as his usual source of care, and also had seven ambulatory physician visits during the study year. He goes to Children's Hospital as his usual source of care for his disability and was admitted there once during the year for dental work. Joseph is an only child. His mother stays home to care for him, but has no relatives or paid help to assist.

Fortunately for the family, the Michigan family subsidy program covers Joseph because the financial eligibility cutoff is $60,000. His father's $44,000 job provides insurance coverage that took care of the hospital bill, except for a small co-payment, but paid almost nothing for ambulatory visits. Joseph lacks a case manager and his parents never received any financial counseling.

The similarity of the developmental problems of these two boys stands in sharp contrast to the differences in the pattern of their financing: Craig's multiple sources of financing and Joseph's single insurance policy. Although there is no substantial difference in the largest expenditure, the hospital bill, for ambulatory care the child with case management has three sources of financing, while the family without case management pays the 98% that insurance fails to cover. In this comparison, the family with most financial need received the most assistance, and thus neither family is currently burdened with medical debt. What financial burden would Craig's family bear without case management?

TABLE 7.7

Autism: Health Care Financing for Individuals with Private Insurance

AVERAGE PAYMENT (N=218, AGE 0-24)

PAYERS	HOSPITAL STAYS[a]	MDs IN PRIVATE PRACTICE	OUT-PATIENT	DENTISTS	DRUGS	SUPPLIES	TOTAL
Family	$15	$70	$60	$50	$50	$45	$290
Insurance	100	55	55	10	40	0	260
Medicaid	185	10	5	5	15	1	220
CSHN[b]	0	0	0	0	0	0	0
Free from provider	125	40	10	10	5	2	190
Other sources	0	3	0	2	1	0	6
Total	$425	$175	$130	$75	$110	$45	$960

Note. Some columns do not sum to totals because data have been rounded to the nearest $5 except payments for supplies and payments for other sources.
[a]Includes attending physician charges.
[b]Title V programs for Children with Special Health Needs.

PROTECTION PROVIDED BY
PRIVATE INSURANCE

A separate examination of the health care expenditures of autistic individuals covered by private insurance shows that policies actually paid roughly one quarter of the total bill, as shown in Table 7.7. Recall that Table 6.1 showed about 20% of families also had Medicaid coverage for their child. Because Medicaid-covered children had higher expenses, Medicaid contributed as much to covering the whole bill as private insurance. Five reasons, mostly concerning the nature of the benefit packages, explain why family total out-of-pocket expenditures were as great as insurance payments: some necessary services were not covered (note the small insurance contribution to payment of dentists); families sometimes failed to submit claims; the annual family deductible happened to affect the payment for this child's services; the reimbursement was low because the insurance fee for the service was below the provider's charge; the family had a standard 20% copayment.

TABLE 7.8

Severe and Profound Mental Retardation: Health Care Financing for Individuals with Private Insurance

	AVERAGE PAYMENT (N=175, AGE 0-24)						
PAYERS	HOSPITAL STAYS[a]	MDs IN PRIVATE PRACTICE	OUT-PATIENT	DENTISTS	DRUGS	SUPPLIES	TOTAL
Family	$40	$90	$60	$10	$60	$200	$460
Insurance	1,250	60	110	5	90	80	$1,590
Medicaid	50	50	30	5	50	40	$220
CSHN[b]	4	3	5	1	3	22	$40
Free from provider	500	100	140	10	20	50	$880
Other sources	220	1	1	0	1	0	$220
Total	$2,060	$300	$350	$30	$220	$390	$3,500

Note. Some columns and rows do not sum to totals because results have been rounded to the nearest $10, except for CSHN, other sources of payment, and dentists.
[a]Includes attending physician charges.
[b]Title V programs for Children with Special Health Needs.

Severely mentally retarded children and young adults fared better in insurance reimbursements, shown in Table 7.8. Insurance companies paid for more than half of the hospital bills, bringing their share of the total bill to half. Although a quarter of individuals were also covered by Medicaid, that source paid very little for hospitalizations and hence less than 10% of the total bill. The average family was spared from paying more than 15% of the total bill thanks to contributions from providers, which totaled about one quarter of the whole expenditure for these six medical services. These two tables show that even when policymakers have solved the problem of providing insurance coverage for everyone, they will not have arranged for insurance to pay the whole bill.

CONCLUSIONS

The overall picture we have examined shows the average family making payments that appear manageable. However, averages are deceptive and hide the few families who pay catastrophically high amounts for the health care of their disabled children. These families deserve special discussion. Their extraordinarily high out-of-pocket payments and medical debt are examined in the next chapter.

Chapter 8
Family Out-of-Pocket Expenses

In a society without universal health insurance and with less than complete coverage for needed services, the issues of self-payment and medical debt receive national attention. A persistent concern among health policy experts is the lifelong financing problems for families with seriously chronically disabled members (Anderson, 1985). The purpose of this chapter is to focus on family out-of-pocket expenses that remain after public and private third-party payments.

The definition of out-of-pocket expenditures we used is from the National Center for Health Statistics (NCHS): the amounts paid by a family that are not reimbursed by insurance or other health care payment programs (Rossiter & Wilensky, 1982). In cases where lack of data prevented knowing whether or not a family had actually paid the balance of a bill paid by insurance, we followed the convention of the NCHS by assuming that the family had paid it.

The findings here are somewhat different from those in previous chapters that treated the child as the unit of analysis and included children in residential placement. Here the unit is the family. Expenditures per family are slightly higher than expenditures per child because about 5% of the families in each disability group had two disabled children. This chapter focuses on children and young adults living at home because these families continued their day-to-day financial responsibility for their children's health care. On a few points, we compare these families with those whose children are in residential placement.

The findings here fit into five broad categories: the size of total family out-of-pocket expenditures for medical and related services; details on out-of-pocket expenditures for related services, such as travel to medical centers and home modification; out-of-pocket payments for habilitative services; the uneven distribution of financial burdens; and the extent of current medical indebtedness.

FINDINGS FROM PREVIOUS STUDIES

The 1977 National Medical Care Expenditure Survey (NMCES) suggests that families will be particularly burdened financially when they include a member reported to be in poor health. Out-of-pocket expenses for young adults in poor health were two-and-a-half times higher than for those in excellent health (Rossiter & Wilensky, 1982). Because this national survey of 14,000 randomly selected households did not contain a sizeable sample of children with serious chronic illnesses or developmental disabilities, we compared our study with the published data on all children in poor or fair health. For such children under age 6, families paid 1.7 times as much out-of-pocket as families where the reported health was good or excellent. Similar findings occur in . older children and young adults. (Rossiter & Wilensky, 1982). As reported earlier (National Center for Health Statistics, 1975), out-of-pocket spending takes a larger share of family income in lower income groups than in higher income groups. The 1987 tax law permitted deductions for medical expenses in excess of 7.5% of gross income, and, as we will see, a few families spent more than that for a single child.

TOTAL OUT-OF-POCKET
EXPENDITURES

The average family with an autistic child under age 18 at home spent about $900 annually on health care and related services, but the local variation was great, ranging among sites from an average of about $500 to about $1,100. Recall from Table 7.1 that the average family spent nearly $300 for six major types of medical services, that are routinely covered by insurance. Merely $25 was the typical family cost for services of allied health professionals and purchases of medical equipment, summarized in Table 5.4, but about $600 was the average family payment for the care services required due to the child's autism that are detailed in Table 5.11: child care, special programs, home modification, damage replacement, travel for medical visits, and respite. The full amount of these last expenses were usually borne by the family alone. In sum, the family's $900 was about half of all health and personal care expenses due to the child's autism. The family's burden was less for young adults, averaging about $500.

For children with severe retardation who live at home, families paid out-of-pocket an average of roughly $1,700 for health care and personal care, which is about one third of the total expenditures. The total out-of-pocket payment varied substantially among sites, ranging from $1,200 to $2,600. These families had almost double the dollar burden of families with an autistic child.

For six basic medical services the families paid about $600, as shown in Table 7.3, and about $150 for services from allied health professionals and durable medical equipment. An additional $900 for all child care services and travel to medical appointments, shown in Table 5.11 brought the average family's total to more than $1,600. The younger the child, the higher the total expenditure, but families have some protection because a higher proportion is covered by third party payers. For young adults with severe retardation, the average family's annual health care expenditure was down to about $750.

At every age, the more medically involved the child, the higher the proportion paid by third parties. This finding is expected because we know from Table 5.10 that retarded children with severe physical disabilities had much higher medical expenses than those able to ambulate. They more frequently required hospitalization and physician services, which are better covered by insurance. As the child used more services, the deductible became a smaller part of the total payments.

We divided the sample of children and young adults with severe and profound mental retardation who were living at home into three categories by their ability to ambulate. For the 60 individuals able to walk half a mile and climb 10 stairs, families had to pay about $500, which was about 55% of the child's total health care bills. For the 45 individuals able to either walk or climb, families had to pay an average of $1,000, about 40% of their total bills; for the 127 who were incapable of both, families paid over $2,000, or about 30% of the total bills.

Insurance here acts in a progressive manner, paying proportionately more for families with greater burdens. However, the most burdened 20% of the families had expenses for the child alone totaling more than 10% of their income. As will be discussed later in this chapter, severe mental retardation was a greater financial burden for families than autism. These computations were based only on families where the child was living at home. The reason for excluding those in residential care was simply that medical events did not directly involve parents when the child lived away from home. But before we begin this analysis it is important to present other dimensions of the financial burden as it impacts on our families.

TRAVEL COSTS FOR MEDICAL VISITS

Respondents were asked to recall all services from health care providers for a three-month period. Along with standard information concerning medical charges, the families reported their expenses for transportation, parking, meals, baby-sitting for other children left at home, and any other related expenses. The respondents reported 254 trips to medical doctors, but reported travel expenses for only 101 trips, or 40%. It is possible that the wording of the questions prompted some parents who drove to appointments to answer that they had no transportation expenses. The majority of parents reporting travel expenses paid less than $2 per visit, one quarter paid more than $6, and one tenth spent more than $12. When we combined transportation costs across all types of visits—including visits to physicians in private practice, outpatient departments, emergency rooms, dentists, and allied health professionals—less than 3% had total travel expenses of more than $100, but the highest was $375.

Families with retarded children had higher travel expenses than families with autistic children, largely due to the higher number of visits, despite the fact that their average cost per trip was slightly lower. Location at a distance from a central city increased the family's travel costs.

Family travel expenses were higher for children in residential placement than for those living at home, in both disability groups. When an autistic child or young adult lived in a residence, about one quarter of the families spent at least $10 in transportation. Nearly half of the families of severely mentally retarded children and young adults in residential placement spent at least $10 in transportation.

Baby-sitting expenses for siblings during these medical appointments were associated with income level of the families. Thirty-three percent of the highest income group in the study had such expenses as compared with an average of 23% for the entire sample comprising all income groups. It is possible that low income families traded baby-sitting services rather than pay for them.

EXPENSES TO MODIFY AND REPAIR THE HOME

The average out-of-pocket expense to modify the physical surroundings totaled about $100 for children with autism, and about $250 for children with severe mental retardation. About 10% of the families have had expenses for home and car modification that exceeded $2,000 per year.

Unfortunately, a few families with autistic children had unusual expenses that did not entirely solve the problems in keeping their children home. One family of three children in suburban Detroit had to make considerable home modifications because their six-year-old son continually tried to run away. They redesigned the interior of the house and placed alarms on the windows and bolts on all the doors.

In another family, an autistic daughter slipped into the kitchen almost daily to dump food and cleaning supplies into a mess on the kitchen floor. She also frequently turned on the faucets, flooding the bathroom. Her mother estimated that the family had paid $400 to repair the bathroom floor, but that a water-damaged rug and a ruined bed accounted for $1,050 in replacement costs that the family was postponing. All together, about 10% of the families spent more than $350 to replace damaged furnishings.

The large expenses of families with children who have severe or profound retardation were typically for purchasing a van that could carry a wheelchair and for one-time interior modifications to permit wheelchair access.

PAYMENT FOR HABILITATIVE SERVICES

The literature on services covered by private health insurance suggests that few private policies adequately cover physical or speech therapy for this population. In addition, we know that not all states pay for those therapies in their Medicaid programs. We found that only about 10% of the children in the study received physical or occupational therapy and only about 5% received speech therapy outside school. Few parents paid for these services. Private and public insurance covered some part of the bill for all but three of the 765 total visits to a physical therapist. More than half the bills were fully paid by Medicaid or by state Crippled Children's Service, or were free from the provider. In the remaining physical therapy visits, private insurance paid part of the bill and the family paid the remainder.

A similar pattern of financing holds for the 282 speech therapy visits. Although 50 visits were paid by the family alone, 46 of these visits were accounted for by 2 families and the remaining 4 visits went to an additional 2 families. Nineteen visits were paid by the family with assistance from private insurance. The great majority, 213 visits, were either paid by Medicaid or by the state Crippled Children's Service, or were free from the provider. Transportation expenses for therapy visits exceeded $8 for only 10% of the families, but 5 families had costs ranging from $30 to $200 dollars.

A plausible explanation of why very few families paid the entire expense of therapies is that if third party payers did not assist, the child did not receive therapies. Recall from Table 4.14 that physical therapy and speech therapy were received by less than one quarter of the children whose primary physicians judged that they would benefit from these services.

THE UNEVEN DISTRIBUTION OF
FAMILY BURDENS

Were the burdens of out-of-pocket expenses equally shared among all families providing direct care or did they disproportionately fall on the shoulders of a small number of families? A reasonable way to answer this question is to examine family expenses as a percentage of family income. On average, families with an autistic child spent 3% of their income and families with a severely retarded child spent roughly 7.5% percent.

As with so many other analyses of services, a small number of families require a great deal of resources and consequently pay more in total dollars and as a percentage of their income. Among families of autistic children, 30% account for about three quarters of these nonreimbursed expenses; and even more dramatically, 10% account for about two-fifths of these expenses. In families who have children with severe and profound mental retardation who often must deal with medically at-risk offspring, we found that 30% had about 85% of the out-of-pocket expenses; and again, 10% accounted for half of all of these expenditures.

Table 8.1 presents another way to view self-payment, by looking at the distribution of the sample according to percentage of family income spent on the health care of children with developmental disabilities.

TABLE 8.1

Out-of-Pocket Medical and Personal Care Expense as Percentage of
Family Income for Children Living At Home

	% OF FAMILIES	
% OF INCOME	AUTISM (N=284)	SEVERE MENTAL RETARDATION (N=254)
<5	83%	65%
5-9.99	10	15
10-14.99	5	10
15-19.99	1	3
≥20	1	7

Less than 5% of their income was spent on the child's health care by about 80% of the families with autistic children and by about 65% of the families with severely retarded children. The proportion of families spending larger amounts tailed off, but about 2% and 10%, respectively, spent more than 15% of their income on the care of their disabled children. At the extreme, about 5% of the families of severely retarded children spent over 25% of their income on health care and personal care.

A remarkable finding is that the proportion of income spent out-of-pocket by families whose children were uninsured was similar to, but not higher than, the average family's spending. This finding leads the inquiry in two directions. First, a further look at the uninsured children shows them to be a heterogeneous group, where the great majority had fewer visits than average; hence their families had fewer out-of-pocket expenses. Second, reflection on the modest share that insurance policies actually paid is supported by the data in Tables 7.7 and 7.8.

To compare the out-of-pocket spending of families caring for disabled children and young adults with national data on family spending, we must return to the narrowly defined medical expenses for hospitals, physicians, allied health care providers, dentists, prescription drugs, durable medical equipment, eyeglasses, and other health supplies. We find that the average family with an autistic child spent about $350 on him or her, but for children with severe retardation, the average was about $800. It is striking to compare the spending on one child with what the average American family spends for the health care of all members. The average family without an elderly person spends less on all members combined, $560. Families with a severely limited member spend somewhat more, $990, and families with a member in poor health spend $1,070 on the entire family. In Table 8.2 we compare mean out-of-pocket expenditures for children and young adults in our study with all American families.

The near poor, those with income between the poverty line and 150% of poverty, spend the most in proportion to their income in both disability categories and among all Americans. The table shows that family spending on medical care for sons and daughters with autism is about $200 per year until the family income rises more than 300% above the poverty line, then it jumps to $400 and then $600.

TABLE 8.2

Annual Out-of-Pocket Expenditures for Families with Public or Private Insurance According to Family Income as a Percentage of Poverty

FAMILY INCOME AS % OF POVERTY LEVEL	AVERAGE ANNUAL FAMILY EXPENDITURES FOR HEALTH CARE		
	U.S. FOR WHOLE FAMILY	FOR CHILD WITH AUTISM (N=284)	CHILD WITH SEVERE MENTAL RETARDATION (N=254)
Average	$741	$350	$800
Below 99%	$300	$200	$200
100-149%	750	175	300
150-199%	886	200	325
200-299%	714	250	875
300-499%	768	400	950
500% +	865	600	1,325

Note. U.S. data is from the National Center for Health Statistics (1987a), *Family Out-of-Pocket Expenditures for Health Care, United States, 1980*, pp. 196-197. Washington, DC: Public Health Service. The 1980 data are adjusted for inflation.

By contrast, family spending on severely retarded children jumps at 200% of poverty and takes another jump at 500% of poverty. It is striking that once family income reaches 200% of poverty, that is, $21,700 in 1986, those with severely retarded children were spending as much for the child as the average family spends on all household members.

There is an important lesson to be learned from this economic view of highly stressed families. Substantial family expenses are omitted in national surveys by the exclusion of personal care due to the disability, travel for medical visits, home modification, and the like. These additional out-of-pocket expenditures increased the total family payments 2.8 times for autism and 2.4 times for severe mental retardation. Any future study of health care expenditures that attempts to shed light on the situation of families of seriously chronically ill and developmentally disabled people would need to build in questions on these burdensome out-of-pocket expenses.

America's expenditures on child care are not supportive of families. All of the expenses incurred by families and charitable organizations to maintain these severely disabled children and young adults in their homes amounted to about $550 annually for autistic offspring and about $950 annually for retarded ones. For physically impaired retarded children, the family has substantial expenses beyond the cost of programs and other caregivers. During the twelve months of the study a few families had substantial expenses for ramps and other home modifications, or to purchase a van to accommodate the wheelchair when they would have preferred a sedan. Private expenditures to keep a child home seem insignificant when contrasted with Medicaid payments to care for a child in residential placement; $16,000 for the typical individual with autism and $27,000 for the individual with severe retardation.

MEDICAL INDEBTEDNESS

The long-term result of high out-of-pocket expenditures is medical debt. About 14% of the families with autistic children and about 20% of the families with severe and profound mentally retarded children had incurred medical debts in caring for their offspring. Half the debts were under $500 per family, but the highest was $300,000.

Among all the families with autistic children, about 1% had medical debts over $2,000 and less than 1% had debts totaling more than 10% of their income. However, among families with severely retarded children, more than 5% had medical debts totaling over $2,000, about 1% had debts over $10,000, and about 4% had debts totaling 10% of their income. Regardless of illness, 31% of those with no insurance had medical debts as opposed to only 10% of those who were privately or publicly insured.

CONCLUSIONS

Although insurance pays a higher proportion of the total bill for more seriously physically disabled children, the family with a typical autistic child still pays about $900 annually for health care and the typical family who has a child with severe retardation is faced with about $1,600 in expenses. The extreme needs of some children, coupled with modest family income, pushed a few families into extraordinary spending—more than 20% of their income.

The implications of these findings are clear concerning future health care financing policy. Proposals to increase assistance to families with severely and profoundly mentally retarded children must seriously consider a targeted approach to those with extreme medical needs. The burdens are many for the few families who must care for children who require enormous amounts of health care as well as educational resources. In the next chapter, we will extend the inquiry into burdens on the families.

Chapter 9

Family Hardships

Severe chronic disability in one's child, like divorce and death, is among the greatest hardships of life. The theme of this chapter is that stresses on the family are numerous and powerful, while societal resources for coping are few and meager. We begin by observing the substantial number of single parent families who are raising children with disabilities. Child care burdens are particularly intense for parents of children who cannot feed themselves, walk about, or ever be left at home alone. Parents find assistance where they can, from the extended family and from community programs. Parents are further burdened when dealing with the health care institutions and educational agencies that provide services to the child. An additional set of stresses usually arises as the child enters adolescence and parents face the fact that their son or daughter will never be capable of living independently.

CHILD CARE NEEDS

Children and young adults with serious developmental disabilities require care far in excess of their healthy peers, yet in our study one quarter of the children living at home did not have two parents to care for them, as shown in Table 9.1.

The single parent households were usually headed by mothers, but a few fathers were coping alone, as were a few grandmothers. For all U.S. children living in metropolitan areas, the proportion is about the same, 23% in single parent homes. Note that the two study groups diverge when the developmentally disabled offspring is a young adult. The autistic adult is more likely to live in a two parent family and the severely retarded adult less likely.

Parents reported whether or not their children, ages 10 to 24 years, could take care of themselves at home alone. Only one third of the members of the study population with autism could take care of themselves, even for a few minutes. Among severely and profoundly retarded offspring, less than one fifth could take care of themselves. Only one quarter of those age 10 to 24 received regular care from someone outside the household, about half from a relative who contributed the service. Among those who had help in child care, the lowest 25% used less than 6 hours a week and the highest 25% used more than 40 hours a week.

TABLE 9.1

Household Structure for Children and Young Adults Living at Home

STRUCTURE	AUTISM	SEVERE MENTAL RETARDATION	U.S. METRO AVERAGE
Under 18 years[a]			
2 Parents	75%	76%	75%
	68-83	67-82	
Single or no parents	25	24	25
	17-32	18-33	
18-24 years[b]			
2 Parents	82%	59%	
	78-93	38-74	
Single or no parents	18	41	

Note. U.S. data is from Bureau of the Census (1987a), Table 9. Percentage ranges represent the next to lowest and next to highest sites.
[a]$N=238$ for autism; 196 for severe and profound mental retardation.
[b]$N=46$ for autism; 58 for severe and profound mental retardation.

The experiences of a farm family in Iowa with three children illustrate the difficulties in obtaining even occasional baby sitting. Sylvia Meadows, age 11, is severely retarded and unable to feed or dress herself. Her brothers, age 4 and 5, are not old enough to care for her. Mrs. Meadows has tried to find an adult to baby-sit, but only teenagers are available. When Sylvia was younger her grandparents cared for her occasionally, but now that she has grown and they have become infirm, they can no longer lift her from her wheelchair. Mr. and Mrs. Meadows wanted to take a one-night trip to a livestock show, but could find no one to stay with their children. A center known to Mrs. Meadows did accept clients for three to four-day stays, but Mrs. Meadows felt it would be hard for her daughter to be away from home that long when all they wanted was a single night's care.

Families bear the financial burden of child care, whether a child goes to the home of a paid sitter, or whether a sitter comes to their home, in no instance did a health insurance policy pay for even part of the child care costs. For about 1% of the 634 children with developmental disabilities in the study, Medicaid paid some child care costs for children at home.

Special camps are the best known summer programs for developmentally disabled children due to their sponsorship by active voluntary associations such as the United Cerebral Palsy Association and the Association for Retarded Citizens. At our study sites about 10 to 15% of the children went to camp. School summer programs, however, served about half the children and young adults. Overnight respite care was received by only about one tenth of the children for a few nights a year.

The usual inconveniences of moving the family residence are amplified by the need to find new providers of services for the disabled child. The average individual in both disability groups under study moved about twice in ten years, a rate that is somewhat lower than the national average. The extreme variation runs from the stable one third who had lived at the same address since birth to the very mobile 5% who had moved more than 8 times in 10 years.

Parents were fundamentally divided over the extent to which they believed that medical services and therapies had helped to improve their children's lives. As reported in Table 9.2, about one third saw little or no improvement, another third saw some improvement, and the last third saw great improvement. The variation in optimism between the parents of children and of young adults was too small to be significant.

TABLE 9.2

**Parents' Beliefs that Medical Care and Therapy Have
Improved Their Child's Life**

| | % OF PARENTS | |
EXTENT OF IMPROVEMENT	AUTISM	SEVERE MENTAL RETARDATION
Under 18 years[a]		
Little or none	39%	34%
	30-49	26-44
Some	36	30
	23-45	27-36
Great	25	36
	14-40	14-44
18-24 years[b]		
Little or none	26%	31%
	0-38	32-57
Some	34	33
	0-57	16-33
Great	40	36
	16-100	33-42

Note. Percentage ranges represent next to lowest and next to highest sites.
[a]N=259 for autism; 239 for severe and profound mental retardation.
[b]N=63 for autism; 91 for severe and profound mental retardation.

INDIRECT COSTS OF THE
CHILD'S DISABILITY

The inability of all young adults with severe or profound mental retardation and most adults with autism to engage in paid employment results in a substantial indirect cost which can be calculated as lifetime earnings foregone. Figure 9.1 addresses another major indirect cost, the lack of employment of mothers. Because they are the primary caretakers, holding a job poses special hardships.

The pattern for mothers of children with severe retardation is consistent across the age range through age 24. About one quarter of the mothers worked full time, about 20% worked part time, and half were not employed. Many interrupted their employment when their children were born and had yet to return. Current data from the Bureau of Labor Statistics on paid employment show mothers with young children working full-time at a rate at least 12 percentage points above the rate of mothers of severely retarded children.

Percent

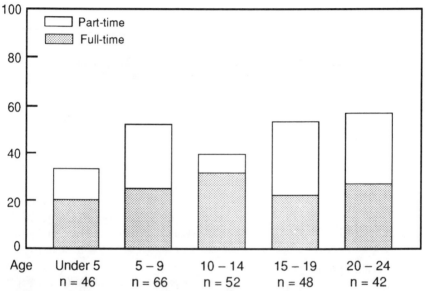

FIGURE 9.1: **Paid employment of mothers of children with severe retardation living at home.**

Nationally, among mothers whose youngest child is between ages 6 and 13, 48% are in full-time paid employment and another 18% are in part-time employment. This places them more than 20 percentage points above the mothers of children with severe retardation. By contrast, mothers whose retarded children are in residential placement are working full time, not far below the national average. The indirect costs in lost income due to the mothers' foregoing work are substantial.

The health care of children in residential placement is completely covered by third party payers, almost entirely by Medicaid. Here, indeed are disincentives for parents to keep children at home: foregoing income from the mother's employment; carrying the health insurance burden instead of relying on the residential placement guarantee of Medicaid coverage; and carrying the physical and financial burdens of daily care for a lifetime.

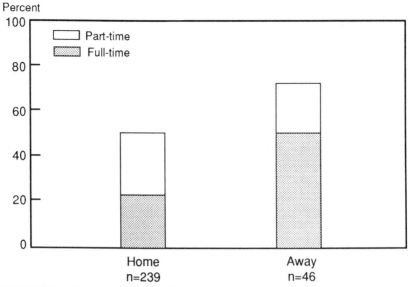

Percent

Part-time
Full-time

Home
n=239

Away
n=46

FIGURE 9.2: Comparison of mothers' paid employment: those whose children with severe or profound mental retardation live at home vs. those whose children are in residential placement.

MENTAL HEALTH SERVICES

An incident from the home of a 17-year-old boy with autism illustrates a tremendous strain from unpredictable violence. One day, the boy's mother used a kitchen knife to chip the ice from the freezing unit of her refrigerator. The next day her son imitated her actions by hacking at the now bare freezing unit with the same knife. His mother, realizing that he did not understand what he had seen, gently tried to stop him. He continued to ruin the refrigerator and then turned the knife on her. In the absence of psychological or pharmacological intervention for the son and lacking psychological support for herself, the fearful mother—a single parent—reluctantly made arrangements for her son to go to a residential institution.

About half the parents of autistic children recalled advice from a physician to obtain psychological help for their autistic child, and most recalled following it. Only about 15% of the parents of children with severe retardation ever received such advice.

The parents and siblings of these children are good candidates for psychological counseling to assist them in maintaining their equilibrium. However, counseling of any variety had never been received by any immediate family member in about two thirds of the families with an autistic child and in about three quarters of the families with a severely retarded child. Within the 12 months studied, some family member had received some kind of counseling in about 15% of the families in the autism group and in about 10% of the families in the mental retardation group.

RESIDENTIAL PLACEMENT

The ultimate step for an overburdened family is to place the severely disabled offspring in residential care. We found 24 individuals in residential placement from the sample of 308 individuals with autism and found 72 in placement out of the 326 who are severely or profoundly retarded. Half of these retarded children and young adults were in large institutions, about one quarter were in group homes and about one quarter were in foster homes.

About two thirds of the offspring in residential care were from single-parent homes. Whether or not only one parent was in the homes of all these children at the time of placement cannot be learned from the cross-sectional data we obtained. If single parent families predominated at the time of placement, clearly residential care is serving particularly needy families.

Among sites, the huge variation in the proportion of individuals in placement appears to depend largely upon the availability of services. A striking fact is that individuals in residential placement differ less from those at home in their functional abilities than in their socioeconomic backgrounds, shown in Table 9.3. The findings on severely retarded children are presented first because the 20% in residential placement, compared to less than 10% of the autistic children, gives more assurance that the findings can be generalized.

One expected difference is that the mean age of all the children and young adults at home was about 12, but for those in placement it was 17. Parents varied greatly in how many years after the child's birth they made the placement decision, but few placed their children in infancy. If parents had based their decisions primarily upon the severity of the child's condition, the data would show that the functional ability of children at home would consistently exceed that of children in placement. This was not the case.

Since more obviously impaired children are diagnosed earlier, one would expect the children in placement to have an earlier age of diagnosis. However, the average age of one year for initial diagnosis holds for the severely retarded children, and the average age of four for the children with autism. In eight functional abilities, from walking to speaking intelligibly, the children in residential placement were no more impaired than the ones at home. In fact, the severely and profoundly retarded individuals in our sample living at home were surprisingly worse in their ability to climb stairs than those in residential placement.

However, a deficit in one key social skill distinguished children in placement from those at home: children in placement sought out the company of other people far less often than children at home. A plausible explanation is that over the years the child's inability to express affection or enjoyment of contact discourages the parents in their persisting efforts to care for their child at home. The causal relation may go in the other direction as well. In placement, fewer demands are placed on the young people to socialize, and

TABLE 9.3

Comparison of Individuals in Residential Placement with Those At Home

CHARACTERISTICS	SEVERE MENTAL RETARDATION		AUTISM	
	PLACEMENT $N=72$	HOME $N=254$	PLACEMENT $N=24$	HOME $N=284$
Child characteristics				
Mean age	17	12**	17	13**
Mean age at diagnosis	1	1	4	4
Male	63%	53%	85%	76%
Can walk ½ mile	24%	35%	96%	94%
Climb 10 stairs	60%	36%**	72%	85%
Feeds self	42%	43%	84%	82%
Goes to toilet by self	44%	36%	64%	67%
Dresses self	31%	21%	41%	42%
Sleeps through night	74%	71%	66%	73%
Speaks intelligibly	4%	7%	24%	22%
Seeks company	37%	54%*	28%	54%**
Medical care has improved child's life	48%	69%*	43%	65%
Household composition				
Mother married	84%	76%	87%	77%
No. other children in home	1.0	0.9	0.9	1.0
Have another disabled child	2%	6%	7%	3%
Socioeconomic characteristics				
Family income in '000s	$36	$28	$53	$39
Mother's years of education	12	12	13	13
Father's years education	13	13	13	14
Families living outside central cities	57%	62%	95%	48%**
White	79%	68%	72%	71%
Mother works full time	55%	47%	45%	34%
Father works full time	97%	80%**	98%	87%
Have medical debts for the child	5%	23%**	15%	8%

*$p < .01$.
**$p < .001$.

the simple enjoyment of socializing decreases through decreased experience. Only a longitudinal study design could answer definitively whether or not failure to seek company occurs as often prior to placement as afterward.

Disbelief that medical care had improved the child's life is another aspect of parental difficulty in finding intrinsic rewards in rearing these children. Parents of both types of children divided into groups of thirds in the extent of improvement they believed resulted from all the medical visits their child had made in the last few years. Table 9.3 groups together the categories "great improvement" and "some improvement," showing that more parents had seen improvement in children whom they kept at home.

In turning to household composition, we find that the families were remarkably alike in these respects: whether or not the mother was married, in the number of siblings who lived at home, and in the presence of additional siblings with the same disabling condition.

Socially advantaged families tended to obtain residential placement for their children. Among children with severe retardation, the mean income of families who placed their children was about $8,000 higher than that of families who did not, but the $14,000 average difference among families with autistic children is not statistically significant because the variation in income was high in both groups. Residence outside a central city was a particularly strong predictor of placement.

A caveat regarding these findings is that the study sites varied so greatly in the proportion of children in residential programs, that site variation alone might greatly influence the findings. However, data from a single site, the Wayne County special education district serving both Detroit and its suburbs, supports the above findings. The 121 individuals with autism and the 60 with severe or profound mental retardation all are served by the same intermediate school district that provides programs up to the 26th birthday. Table 9.4 shows the same results as for the multi-site study: children in placement were older but not more severely disabled, and, in the autism groups, their families came overwhelmingly from the suburbs.

TABLE 9.4

**Comparison of Individuals in Wayne County, Michigan,
by Living Arrangement**

CHARACTERISTICS	HOME	PLACEMENT
Autism	$N=110$	$N=11$
Mean age	14 years	20 years
Mean age at diagnosis	5 years	10 years
Can walk ½ mile	90%	100%
Live in the suburbs	40%	90%
Severe Mental Retardation	$N=48$	$N=12$
Mean age	13 years	19 years
Mean age at diagnosis	1 years	0.9 years
Can walk ½ mile	10%	50%
Live in the suburbs	40%	40%

The paucity of support services for young adults in their parents' homes exacerbates the burden on the families. Fewer families used overnight respite care than placed their child in a permanent residence. Policy recommendations on child care as well as on health care are the topics of chapter 10.

Chapter 10
Policy Recommendations on the Financing of Care

This study has pinpointed substantial problems of families in obtaining health care for their children with developmental disabilities. Conservatively stated, our recommendations are based primarily on the data that we collected, supplemented by data from national data sets. The recommendations apply to two categories of seriously developmentally disabled children: those with autism and those with severe or profound mental retardation. In addition, they provide the framework for broader recommendations for children with other serious chronic conditions and illnesses. Because we believe that many of the problems we address are generic to chronically ill children, we have kept this diversity in mind in exploring policy options.

The policy options considered here take full account of efforts to contain health care costs, which now consume 11.5% of the gross national product. The discussion draws upon policy analysis techniques applied to disability policy in a comprehensive study by Brewer and Kakalik (1979) and later presented in a generic form in Brewer and deLeon (1983). We begin with a statement of goals. Through this analysis we have drawn useful data from the policy analysis by Bob Griss (1988, 1989) of the World Disability Institute. The organization of the specific recommendations, first around private sector solutions and then around public sector solutions, follows the structure of the insightful Brookings study on care for the disabled elderly (Rivlin & Wiener, 1988).

The reader who wishes to obtain more background on national policies to promote child health will find key works from the 1980s both in the literature on children's policy and in the literature on health policy. *Within Our Reach* (1988) by Schorr and Schorr is a vivid, thoughtful updating of the findings of the Public Health Service's Select Panel for the Promotion of Child Health (1981). Documentation of the declining resources during the Reagan administration is provided by an Urban Institute study (Kimmich, 1985), and the Children's Defense Fund (1989) proposes a national agenda for the betterment of children.

On the health care system, the dimensions of the problems are traced by a number of edited works (Ginzburg, 1985; Lewin, 1985; Schramm, 1987) and the report on objectives for 1990 from the Office of Disease Prevention and Health Promotion of the Public Health Service (1986). The National Academy of Sciences report (1989) describes a research and intervention agenda to reduce childhood mental and developmental disorders. Two thoughtful monographs covering the intersection of children's issues and health issues are the works edited by Walker and Richmond (1984) and by Stein (1989). Kohrman's chapter (1989) in Stein's book provides a good introduction to issues in financing care for chronically ill children.

We address three basic problems. One, a small but significant proportion of disabled children lack health insurance. Two, among children who have insurance, most have policies that do not cover needed services. Three, insurance policies fail to protect families from catastrophic medical expenses. A consequence of these three insurance gaps is that some children are not receiving appropriate health care.

Of the children we studied, about 30% of those under age 6 failed to receive regular medical checkups, 40% at all ages failed to receive dental checkups, and at least 50% and perhaps 80% failed to receive physical therapy when their physician deemed it worthwhile. The majority of children with complex medical conditions were not receiving case management services. The good news is that private health insurance coverage of home care is rapidly expanding, particularly when home care is less expensive than hospital or institutional care. In considering policy alternatives, we identify proposals requiring low, moderate, and substantial public expenditure.

GOALS OF REFORM

For clarity, we begin with a brief statement of seven goals which we believe should be the basis of reform.

First, *primary prevention is the most desirable solution to the problems of developmental disability.* Long-term research in mapping the human genome can be expected to result in substantial new opportunities for prevention. The immediate future may bring new medical knowledge piecemeal that can prevent deleterious effects of specific genetic deficits, such as has long been achieved by protecting infants with phenylketonuria from severe mental retardation through proper nutrition. Without assuming imminent breakthroughs in the technology of prevention, we believe that systematic application of existing knowledge can assist parents to make informed choices in family planning and can promote excellence in prenatal care.

Second, *the birth of a seriously developmentally disabled child should be treated as a normal risk for which insurance provides protection.* Normally, raising healthy children does not impoverish a family. Neither should raising a child with a severe disability. The costs of health care and personal care for a child who is seriously disabled should not be borne solely by the immediate family, but shared widely through an insurance system in which payments from all are used to cover the risk to a few. Americans insure their homes against fire, their cars against collision, their valuable packages against loss in the mail, and themselves against hospitalization. We believe that insurance is a sound mechanism for reducing the hardship of fundamental inequities. Further, we believe that if private insurance does not cover the risk, public insurance must.

Third, *the health care requirements of these children should be viewed broadly so as to include personal care and family support necessary because of their disabilities.* In the routine circumstances of a five-year-old boy free of chronic illness and disability, an annual medical checkup may be the only health care service he needs and is entirely distinct from his parents' need for a Saturday night baby sitter. However, the medically involved child, for example, a fifteen-year-old boy with spina bifida, would be likely to benefit from corrective surgery, physical therapy, installation of a home elevator, and a sitter who can perform clean, intermittent catheterization. We believe that it is appropriate to regard all of these services as health care because, in the absence of a health condition, none of them would be necessary for a 15-year-old. Case management should coordinate the whole gamut of necessary care.

Fourth, *financing should promote family-centered care.* To state the case in bold terms, the family should be regarded as the unit for receiving services. The tendency of Americans in the late 20th century to look at individuals without seeing them as members of families results in a distorted view. Specifically, it is unrealistic to believe that excellent services are being provided to a severely retarded and physically disabled child when he receives appropriate schooling but his parents and siblings obtain no assistance in bearing the physical, mental, emotional, and social burdens of his care. The Association for the Care of Children's Health has put forward a comprehensive overview of family-centered care that is itemized in checklists for all participants in the child's care (Shelton, Jeppson, & Johnson, 1987). In the empowerment of parents, they should be able to call upon services to assist them in keeping their disabled son or daughter in their home beyond childhood. The natural desire of parents to nurture their children during their growing years should be especially encouraged for children whose progress is measured in centimeters. Whenever families decide that they can no longer bear the burden of care, the transition to a residential placement should be facilitated.

Fifth, *the transition to services for adults should be smooth.* Medical knowledge can now predict the usual course of most disabilities and the pattern of likely service needs. Our data can contribute to the formation of a profile of utilization and costs for health care services at different points in the life cycle. Using this profile, planners can predict what is needed. Young adults with serious, chronic conditions continue to need appropriate programs and personal care after they have completed school. Some forward-looking special education directors have attempted to piece together programs for their severely disabled graduates, but the heavily burdened education system cannot be expected to fill this policy vacuum. Systematic commitment of resources is needed at state and federal levels. In its absence, parents are left in uncertainty about how their disabled sons and daughters will be cared for in the decades ahead.

Sixth, *financing should be administratively simple.* The administrative costs of private insurance for 1987 were $18.7 billion out of a total of $157.8 billion

(Letsch, Levit, & Waldo, 1988). Not only is 12% a large proportion to divert from direct services to administration, but the complexity of insurance criteria for determining the dollar amounts policies cover prevents employers and consumers from making informed choices. The overlapping public and private systems use complicated and conflicting criteria for who is eligible, what services are covered, and how much is paid for different services. The recent proliferation of competing health maintenance organizations, preferred provider organizations, and the like has increased complexity. Because consumers and providers must spend enormous effort to keep informed on policies of third party payers, the great majority act in ignorance.

Seventh, *financing should promote cost effective health care.* Total health care spending in 1989 is expected to exceed $600 billion and, at 11.5% of the gross national product, is still climbing. This proportion, greater than at any time in American history and greater than in any other country, may be seen as an aberration that requires correction. Cost containment issues are so dominant that national health insurance is now frequently discussed as a mode of controlling the growth of the health care industry, rather than as a means for improving access.

In the cycle of American political discourse, national health insurance has surfaced three times as a realistic policy alternative, in the 1910s, in the 1930s, and in the 1960s (Starr, 1982). Apparently in the 1990s it may again approach political feasibility. We believe that a national health plan can be more easily shaped to promote the health of children with chronic illness and disabilities than can the present complicated private and public system. If current policy options are to be weighed in terms of how they affect children's health in the long run, then they could be judged by how well they facilitate children becoming the next age group to be covered by a national health insurance system. Rather, we have chosen to take a short-term view that assesses options in terms of their direct benefit to children with disabilities.

PRIVATE SECTOR STRATEGIES
FOR REFORM

Private sector strategies are important because "the Reagan revolution" has set a climate of opinion that questions government spending for social welfare programs, and the current budget deficit pits every new spending proposal against the agreed national priority of reducing that deficit. Further, state and local governments are creatively finding ways to turn over to the private sector a variety of public services (Savas, 1987). What state and federal legislation would entice or coerce private insurers to change their policies so that they more fully meet the needs of chronically disabled children?

Problem 1: Lack of Health Insurance

"Society has an ethical obligation to ensure equitable access to health for all," is the conclusion reached by the President's Commission for the Study of Ethical Problems in Medicine (1983, p.29). The present realities are succinctly stated by Bob Griss (1989):

> In the absence of an entitlement to health care, persons with disabilities or chronic illness are squeezed between a private health insurance system which is designed to charge according to the probability of risk, and a public health care system which subsidizes health on the basis of age, poverty status, family structure, and an inability to work, rather than on the basis of health care needs (p.2).

From the perspective of private insurance, uninsured children may be grouped into three categories: children whose parents are unemployed; children whose parents are employed yet do not have family coverage; and children with high expenditures making them "uninsurable."

In our study, about 90% of the uninsured children had employed parents. Like most uninsured children, the substantial majority in our study came from intact families where the father held full-time employment. Only one severely retarded infant out of the 34 uninsured children had expenses as high as $16,000, while 4 others had expenses in the $1,000 to $5,000 range. Clearly, for these children with developmental disabilities, the problem is the working uninsured.

Each of these classes of uninsured requires a somewhat different solution. When employment is the major source of health insurance, children suffer particular hardship if their parents are jobless in the long term or even intermittently. Private insurance can be acquired for the children of parents who are unemployed through the purchase of an individual policy. However, insurance companies use actuarial criteria to deny insurance outright or to provide a substandard plan that excludes services or charges a higher premium. The Congressional Office of Technology Assessment (1988) estimated that commercial insurers provided substandard policies to 20% of the applicants and denied insurance to 8%; Blue Cross and Blue Shield provided substandard policies to 9% and also denied 8%; and HMOs contracted to provide substandard service to 3% and denied 24%. The irony is that the individuals who need insurance most cannot obtain it.

The proportion of dependents who are covered by the breadwinner's insurance policy has dropped from 34.3% of the American population under age 65 in 1979 to 31.4% in 1985 (Griss, 1989). This is a consequence of a trend noted in Figure 6.2 and 6.3. Firms have raised employee premiums and copayments for family coverage faster than for individual employee coverage in their efforts to keep down fringe benefit costs.

The insurance term "uninsurable" refers to an individual with a high risk of very high expenditures. If the group across which this individual's costs are spread is large, the risk can be absorbed easily. However, the insurance industry has virtually abandoned community rating, the system created by Blue Cross that spread risk most widely by considering all people insured by a firm in a large geographic area to belong to a single risk pool.

Instead, experience rating has long been used by commercial insurers and is now used by Blue Cross. Under experience rating, a single employer's workers and their dependents form their own risk pool. If in a given year the employees of a firm experience the birth of several multiply impaired infants, on the basis of that experience of higher medical expenses, the insurance company will raise the premium. A small risk pool concentrates the burden for rare disabilities and illnesses in a highly inequitable way. The smaller the firm, the more likely that anyone with high expenses is to be considered "uninsurable." Approximately seven million people actually covered by insurance would be considered "uninsurable" if they sought to purchase a new policy, according to a recent estimate from the Department of Health and Human Services (Griss, 1989). State mandates are the major way in which insurance coverage is compelled for those described as uninsurable.

Mandates to Employers

In 1974 Hawaii became the first state to require firms to provide insurance to employees who work more than 20 hours per week, but coverage for dependents was optional (Griss, 1989). The Massachusetts plan, to take effect in 1992, has been dubbed the "play or pay option." It requires employers with five or more employees to provide health insurance or else pay a surcharge of 12% of each full-time worker's annual earnings up to a maximum of $1,680 into a fund that will be used to insure employees and their families. Massachusetts will also provide tax credits as start-up incentives.

Current federal legislation introduced by Senator Edward Kennedy, Chairman of the Labor and Human Resources Committee, called the Basic Health Benefits for All Americans Act (S. 768), would require employers to pay up to 80% of the premium for all workers and their dependents who work more than 17½ hours per week. Individuals not covered by private insurance, Medicaid, or Medicare would be eligible for phased-in public coverage from the states under federal guidelines. The mandatory benefits package would include prenatal and well-child care, hospital and physician services. In a related effort, Congressman Peter Stark, Chairman of the Ways and Means Subcommittee on Health, has introduced the Employee Health Benefits Improvement Act (H.R. 4951), which requires employers either to provide insurance or to contribute to a state-wide health insurance pool from which anyone could buy insurance at no more than 150% of the price for a standard group policy (Griss, 1989). As of this writing, these and other pieces of legislation are on hold because Congress is considering the comprehensive recommendations of the Pepper Commission, discussed toward the end of this chapter.

State governments have not hastened to follow Hawaii's lead because they recognize that mandating health benefits makes their states more costly and less desirable locations for business. Likewise, the Kennedy bill has not yet been passed after reintroduction because lawmakers are reluctant to drive marginal firms out of business or to add to the high price of American goods in international trade.

The interests of chronically disabled children would be served directly by any of these mandates that end the lack of insurance for the small fraction who are uncovered. Indirectly, all children with chronic conditions would benefit because once health insurance is provided for the 34 million who now lack it, policy attention can be directed to the gross inadequacy of the standard benefits for individuals with disabilities. Underinsurance is the pervasive problem. For families with private insurance, Table 7.7 shows that on average only 30% of the autistic patient's total bill for hospitalizations, physicians, dentists, drugs, and supplies was paid by insurance, while Medicaid and provider charity shared 40%, leaving 30% to the family. Insured families who had children with severe retardation were better served by their policies, which covered about half of the bill, leaving the average family to pay 15% (Table 7.8).

Two other federal laws mandating specifics of insurance coverage are relevant to disabled children. The Health Maintenance Organization Act of 1973 sets conditions requiring employers to offer the option of joining an HMO if a qualified one exists in the area. The 1986 Consolidated Budget Reconciliation Act (COBRA) requires firms with more than 20 employees to permit those leaving employment to continue full coverage for 18 months as long as they pay all premiums, including the employer's share. These two federal mandates could become the thin end of the wedge for the entry of more effective ways to structure private health insurance. Federal mandates could replace state mandates.

State Insurance Regulation

States, through their insurance commissioners, are the level of government that traditionally has regulated the insurance industry. However, they do not regulate the one third of the industry composed of large corporations insuring themselves.

A word about the rapid changes in the insurance industry is necessary here to explain the limits of state authority. The double-digit inflation of the late 1970s prompted big businesses to switch from paying insurance companies millions in premiums (upon which the insurance company accrued the interest) to becoming self-insured and hiring insurance companies to provide merely administrative services. A major consequence of self-insurance is that businesses escape state regulation because they are regulated by federal legislation, the Employee Retirement Income Security Act of 1974 (ERISA), which explicitly excludes self-funded plans from state insurance regulation (Cohodes, 1986).

The highly competitive and fragmented health insurance industry, when measured in 1986 by the dollar volume of premium payments, was composed of the following major components: 32% Blue Cross and Blue Shield, 25% commercial group and individual policies, 15% commercial stop-loss policies for self-insured businesses, 21% self-insured business plans, and 7% HMO and other prepaid plans (Health Care Financing Administration, 1987). The self-insured proportion, as of 1986, was composed of both the 21% direct business plans and the 15% stop-loss policies, which are a type of reinsurance that employers take against potentially huge totals in claims. Thus, 36% of the people with group health insurance were unprotected by state regulation, and that proportion is still growing, estimated in 1990 to be half.

State mandates to insurance companies, through their insurance commissioners or state legislatures, have become more powerful in protecting people insured directly by insurance companies, but do not affect people whose policies are carried by their employers as self-insurance. Because ERISA preempts state legislation, states now do not regulate the 36% of the insurance business that stems from the directly self-insured and reinsurance for the self-insured.

Prior to 1965, there were only two state mandates, but by 1986 the total reached 645 (Griss, 1989). An early mandate crucial to the protection of children with chronic conditions was promoted by the American Academy of Pediatrics to cover infants from the moment of birth, not after a waiting period. A recent mandate adopted by 34 states permits parents to cover their adult mentally or physically impaired offspring if they live with them and are economically dependent. Minnesota requires that disabled dependents be included in all policies (Griss, 1989).

A change in parental health insurance typically causes hardship for disabled children. Recall that about 20% of the parents of severely retarded children had encountered refusals and limitations in the insurance they could purchase, as did about 10% of the parents of autistic children. In addition to the federal mandate in the 1986 COBRA that entitles employees to continue their coverage after leaving a job, some states now require an insurance company that is newly providing coverage to a firm to include every member who was covered by the previous policy (Griss, 1989). Piece by piece, state by state, advocates for people with disabilities have forced insurance companies to take risks they seek to avoid, but we judge that the problem remains serious.

Our policy recommendation on state mandates is that Congress permit piecemeal progress to continue in the states by amending ERISA so that states have the authority to regulate the insurance offerings of self-insured businesses. We recognize that amending ERISA is a major undertaking for a number of reasons. Because there is joint jurisdiction in Congress, the legislation has to be referred to committees sequentially, in the Senate to both the Labor and Human Resources Committee and the Finance Committee. This is a cumbersome process. Because ERISA has not been opened up for fundamental changes, many proposals have accumulated that are opposed by business and many opposed by labor. Amending ERISA is like opening Pandora's box; a swarm of interests have other amendments to propose. Whenever the day comes for a major overhaul of ERISA, the proponents for children who are disabled and chronically ill should be ready with amendments that have wide support.

Congressional failure to place self-insured firms under state regulation guts state power to control the health insurance industry. A comprehensive change would place the self-insured firms under state jurisdiction and, at the same time, create federal mandates to make insurance more suitable for children with chronic conditions. Consequently, all payers would absorb the costs of health care for the uninsurable.

This line of thinking is not foreign to insurance executives. At a 1989 Brookings public policy seminar, Robert Laszewski, the chief operating officer for group markets of Liberty Mutual, stated a view that emphasizes the power of mandates: while no single insurer alone can afford to remove restrictions because the high-risk individuals who were previously uninsured would flock to that company, all companies, including the self-insured, could work under new federal mandates that forbid preexisting condition clauses and lifetime caps of $100,000.

Family Health Insurance Based on School Enrollment

An innovative policy proposal by Steven Freedman and his colleagues of the Institute for Child Health Policy is that state school systems play the role of employer by offering health insurance policies to their pupils and their families (Freedmann, Klepper, Duncan & Bell, 1988). This proposal addresses systematically the problem that 25 of the 34 million uninsured are school children and their parents. The strengths of the proposal are that a system set up on a state-wide basis would create a very large risk pool and that children and young adults are generally in good health. The weaknesses of the system are that the family would pay the premium directly (unlike group insurance where the premium is part of an employer's fringe package) and that it would not cover preschool children.

Public Subsidies for Private Insurance

One suggestion for enabling low income families to purchase private health insurance is that a government agency assist families to pay the premiums. Charitable organizations are restricted to this approach because they lack legislative and regulatory powers. A government, however, has alternatives.

Through tax policy it can regulate the market so that employers and private insurance companies have incentives to provide insurance to the formerly uninsured. Through legislation and administrative regulation, government can require compliance.

Another alternative, a state reinsurance mechanism, would place on state governments the risk of high cost for an individual's health care. The fundamental flaw of government reinsurance to insurance firms is that it separates the responsibility to pay costs from authority to control them. In the health care system as a whole, the major cause of medical price inflation has been the lodging of payments in third party payers, which are separate from consumers and from service providers, who determine costs.

Financial Counseling

The provision of financial counseling is a low-cost, decentralized approach that will alleviate the burden of some families. The National Hemophilia Foundation encourages staff at hemophilia treatment centers to give systematic financial guidance to parents along the lines developed by David Linney of the Great Lakes Hemophilia Foundation. Linney also educates insurance companies in how to include new medical procedures in their coverage. Cooperation with the insurance industry and sound financial counseling are largely responsible for the fact that in our study of children with hemophilia we found that 60% of their medical expenses were paid by private insurance. Consider, however, that insurance covered only about 20% of the strictly medical expenses for both groups of developmentally disabled children in this study, whereas the national average for Americans of all ages is 31% (Griss, 1989).

When experts in financial counseling know the fine points of the insurance industry, families can work the system to benefit their children. For example, Blue Cross organizations maintain their nonprofit status by holding an annual 30-day period of open enrollment. At that time, they do not employ medical underwriting criteria to exclude anyone. An effective technique of the hemophilia centers is to use unrestricted gifts to the centers to purchase individual Blue Cross policies for uninsured men and boys from low-income families. Another technique of the centers is to prepare parents to anticipate when their sons will no longer be dependents. If parents purchase individual policies for their sons a year before they will need them, then the year's exclusion of coverage for a preexisting condition will have elapsed by the time the son needs the policy.

State High-risk Health Insurance Pools

Analogous to health insurance high-risk pools are motor vehicle insurance high-risk pools. Individuals who are rejected by insurance companies can obtain health insurance through a state pool for a premium set at a reasonable price, typically 150% of the standard premium. The gap between the total premiums collected by the pool and the total it pays in benefits is divided among all insurance companies doing business in the state. ERISA prevents states from requiring self-insured corporations to participate, thus narrowing the base for spreading the high risk.

Some states also subsidize the losses that inevitably occur as high-risk individuals are grouped together. As of 1987, 15 states had created high-risk pools, but they tended to enroll only a tiny fraction of their target population. Minnesota and North Dakota are outstanding, with respective enrollments of 33% and 25% of the estimated numbers of high risk individuals who lack insurance. More typical of pools are the 5% enrollment in Indiana and 2% in Florida. Two states, Wisconsin and Maine, have created separate risk pools for individuals with preexisting conditions, isolating high-cost individuals rather than spreading the risk.

The most comprehensive discussion that is favorable to high-risk pools has been issued by an organization called Communicating for Agriculture (Trippler, 1987), and an insightful critique is presented by Griss (1989). Here we note that the benefit of high-risk pools to families of disabled children is that they do obtain coverage, although at a high cost for premium, deductible, and copayments. The pools benefit hospitals by reducing the amount of uncompensated care and employers by keeping premiums down. The advantage to insurance companies is that they can refer rejected applicants to the pool. The experience with auto insurance suggests that companies in fierce competition will refuse to renew an ever larger proportion of individual policies on the grounds of above-average risk and will divert them in good conscience to the high-risk pools.

Problem 2: Insurance Fails to Cover Needed Services

This section begins with standard health care needs and ends with a discussion of long-term care needs. The most glaring omission of services from private insurance coverage is created by the standard preexisting condition clause; that is, an illness or disability that an individual had prior to acquiring a policy will not be covered until a year has elapsed. Because today's health insurance system was begun by hospitals to keep up occupancy during the Depression, private insurance began by covering hospitalization. The inclusion of physician services is relatively recent; as late as 1965 half the policies were for hospital care alone. Today's policies do not adequately cover habilitative services and therapies. Case management is particularly appropriate for medically complex cases, but case managers who report to insurance companies have a first responsibility to contain costs.

We will take up first these commonly criticized failings of the typical private policy, an then discuss home care, respite, day programs and other crucial services for the child and family. The standard criticism of private insurance for failing to cover needed services almost never notes the failure to cover day programs, respite, and child care because these types of services do not fall within a narrow definition of health care. The two-point argument that we will advance is that (a) the current interest in extending private insurance to cover long-term care for the disabled elderly can stimulate parallel discussions regarding children and young adults with severe disabilities; and (b) home care services of all sorts, which are the alternative to residential care, ought to be financed by the same funding sources as residential care. The mechanisms that could induce private insurers to cover needed services are the "stick" of mandates and the "carrot" of favorable tax treatment.

Uncovered Services

Preventive medical and dental care are not well covered by private insurance. In our study the 30% percent of children under age 6 who failed to have an appropriate frequency of monitoring visits by physicians included many children covered by private health insurance. If families hold a typical insurance policy that excludes coverage for health maintenance visits, the parents receive no financial inducement to take the child for a medical checkup.

Our data clearly document inadequate use of ambulatory dental services. A year or more elapsed between visits for about 40% of the children with autism and with severe mental retardation. Looking solely at members of the study population covered by private health insurance, we see that their policies paid on average only 15% of their dental bills. Parents have told us of postponing dental work until they finally had to send their autistic child to a hospital. We were able to identify dental work as the reason for at least 30% of all hospital stays by young adults with autism. Consistent dental care enhances health and is cost effective. For these children, early treatment prevents the need for sedation and even hospitalization to perform procedures that are relatively simple in children who are cooperative. The per capita expenditure on ambulatory dental care was about $60 for the sample of children and young adults with autism, but the per capita expenses for hospitalizations for dental procedures were far higher.

Therapies of all types are less well covered by insurance than are physicians' services. When occupational, physical, speech, and other habilitative therapies and all psychological services are considered together, only about 15% of the children with autism received any of these services outside of school, as did only about 20% of the children with severe mental retardation. Most of this minority who receive therapy have insurance plans covering therapeutic services.

Long-term care needs should be included in comprehensive thinking about children with severe developmental disabilities. Just as fresh thinking about long-term care for the elderly includes new ways to expand home care, so thinking about children with chronic conditions should include many varieties of child care and family services (Fox & Neiswander, 1989). The majority of older children with severe developmental disabilities cannot be left at home alone, even for fifteen minutes. This burden of constant attention requires occasional alleviation, but the only alleviation that is financially supported is residential placement. From the parents' perspective, placement is cost effective because they pay nothing after the first month. Medicaid eligibility rules deem that the family income belongs to the child during the first month, but thereafter, only the child's own income and assets, typically nil, share in the payment. The paradox of this situation is that home care is cost effective from a societal perspective but costly to the family, because they must either find free caregivers among relatives or pay the whole bill. If a single source were to pay for both long-term residential care and for its substitutes, the payer would have monetary incentive to provide a range of child care, home care, day programs, and respite services as alternatives to residential care.

The national trend of deinstitutionalization since 1967 has slowed the numbers of children and young adults entering institutions. The 1977 total of about 91,000 children and youth under the age of 21 in public and private institutions for mental retardation fell to about 60,000 in 1982 and to about 48,500 in 1987 (Lakin, 1989). This massive shift has not been accompanied by a corresponding increase in family support services.

If private insurers were to offer a special package of home and residential care for severely developmentally disabled dependents, there would be no buyers except parents of disabled children. The low incidence of serious developmental disabilities encourages parents to ignore the possibility. No one wants to plan ahead to safeguard against the birth of a disabled child, much less to safeguard that fictional offspring's care as an adult. The problems of providing insurance for children with disabling chronic conditions are similar to developing insurance products to cover long-term care for the elderly. It is extremely high priced because insurers fear adverse selection, that those who anticipate using it are disproportionately among the purchasers. Less than 500,000 long-term care policies had been issued by 1987 for a population of 28 million elderly and 100 million middle-aged adults. (Rivlin & Wiener, 1988). Private insurance for long-term care during the last years of life could work if a cross-section of the working age population purchased such policies. Unfortunately, the children who need long-term care have not spent years in the work force contributing to the fund from which their benefits will later be drawn. Unlike the elderly, they cannot prepay for later use.

We raise child care and long-term care as issues for private insurance in order to open this payment source for exploration. Several lines of argument converge to suggest that private insurance has the potential to assume a new role. Severely disabled and chronically ill children have child care needs that are markedly different from the needs of the average child. Private insurance has expertise in financing the health care needs of people with neurophysiological conditions. Recently, insurance has gained experience in funding alternatives to institutional care. The situation of ventilator-assisted children is a clear example of insurance companies financing creative, individually tailored home care services to permit these children to live with their families rather than in the hospital. If private insurance were to become a payer for long-term care for the disabled, the creativity of market competition would develop new services as alternatives to residential placement.

However, there is neither a market for such insurance nor the political will to mandate it. Private insurance will provide long-term care for people with developmental disabilities only if governments require it. State governments are unlikely to mandate home and residential care because a large insurance benefit package increases the cost of running a business, a drawback mentioned earlier. Since mandates to private insurance are highly unlikely, achieving a balance between home care and residential care will come, if at all, through public sector reforms.

State and Federal Mandates to Insurers

The mandates discussed earlier were to employers, requiring them to provide insurance under certain conditions. Mandates to insurers typically regulate the contents of the benefits package. Forbidding preexisting condition clauses is essential to the health care of disabled children. Historically, insurers have given equity as the reason for not covering services for the maladies people have when they acquire the insurance and requiring them to wait for coverage, typically a year. If healthy people get along without insurance until they fall acutely ill, their purchase at the time of sickness will thrust an unfair burden on healthy people who have contributed to insurance for years. States are beginning to issue mandates in this area. One forbids an insurance company from imposing a preexisting condition clause on a person who is already carrying insurance and then changes policies, due to a change of jobs.

Recently states have increased their mandates to insurance companies, requiring them to offer plans that provide benefits for preventive, habilitative, and rehabilitative care (Blue Cross and Blue Shield, 1990). Mandates of services for well-child care are made by 11 states. Thirty-four states mandate that policyholders be allowed to continue coverage for their adult children who are too disabled to work. Physical therapy is mandated by 6 states, occupational therapy by 3, speech and hearing therapy by 4, and orthotic and prosthetic devices by 5. By contrast, far more states require that Medicaid cover these services and equipment. A growing number of states mandate services that assist not only the disabled individual but the whole family: 27 require coverage of mental health services, 17 home health care, and 3 long-term care.

222

Problem 3: Insurance Does Not Protect All Families from Large Out-of-Pocket Expenses

As reported in Chapter 8, among families with an autistic child, about 5% had out-of-pocket health care expenditures for that child alone amounting to more than 10% of the family income. The situation is much harsher for families of children with severe or profound retardation. About 19% had expenses above 10% of family income, and about 4% had expenses more then 25% of family income.

Annual Caps and Life-time Limitations

Two practices of private insurance companies exacerbate the burden on families of high-cost children. An annual cap fixes the dollar amount that insurance will pay for a particular type of service, such as psychological counseling, or for all services. A lifetime limitation can be set on particular services, such as 30 days of psychiatric hospitalization, or on the total dollars of reimbursement, such as a $100,000 maximum during the child's life. These practices cast a dim light on the insurance industry's stance that ordinary insurance policies are a mechanism to share risk rather than to provide prepaid health care. Historically, insurance has not covered health maintenance visits to physicians on the grounds that the need for such care is not a risk but a certainty, and hence individuals ought to budget to cover them and let insurance cover unanticipated large expenses for risks such as hospitalization. However, when employers and private insurance firms use caps and lifetime limitations, they push the very highest risks back on families. State or federal mandates could prohibit both annual caps and lifetime limits.

State Mandates of Stop-loss Policies

A stop-loss policy does for a family what annual caps do for an insurance company. A stop-loss policy sets an upper limit for the family's total annual out-of-pocket payments, say $3,000. After the family pays that amount, insurance will cover 100% of all legitimate claims. The short-lived Medicare catastrophic illness protection had both an overall stop-loss limit of $2,146 and three lower limits for specific services.

By way of summarizing these various options for reform of private insurance, we note that each one proposes adjustments of a complex system that improves the services but makes the system slightly more complicated. A fundamental failing of private insurance is that its complexity prevents consumers from becoming well informed. A basic political problem is that each state that mandates insurance benefits might drive up the cost of doing business in the state to the extent that new businesses go elsewhere and insurance companies stop writing policies in the state. The experience with high-risk pools for motor vehicle collision insurance provides numerous examples of insurance firms withdrawing from doing business in individual states.

PUBLIC SECTOR STRATEGIES
FOR REFORM

While private sector strategies tend to be piecemeal adjustments to induce the market to provide services to people who lack the purchasing power to command them, public sector strategies can range from overhauling the system to filling the gaps. Having already examined the problems of lack of insurance, inadequacy of services covered, and catastrophic family expenses, we will probe each policy option for its adequacy in addressing all of these problems. We will begin with the most comprehensive proposal and afterward discuss more modest reforms.

Expansion of Medicaid Coverage for Poor Children

Medicaid, during its first two decades, served primarily children on welfare. Congress has begun a process of extending state options for eligibility along three dimensions: the child's age, the family income, and increasing optional state services that are later transformed into mandatory ones. In 1986 the Reconciliation Act created an avenue to Medicaid benefits outside of the only previous route, obtaining federal income support (AFDC, SSI or SSDI). The new option permitted states to provide Medicaid coverage to all children whose family income was below the poverty line. The age of eligibility for poor children began as an option for pregnant women and infants but now reaches to age 8. Eligibility for pregnant women and infants went first to those with incomes at 100% of poverty and then to 185%.

A provision of the 1987 Reconciliation Act provides states the option of covering children up to age 8 whose family earnings are at the poverty line. Overall, the Medicaid coverage changes in the 1980s occurred piecemeal; the federal government providing a state option in one year became the federal mandate the next. The Reconciliation Act of 1989 brought a dramatic increase by requiring the states to cover pregnant women and children under age 6 up to 133% of poverty. As states expand their Medicaid programs to serve more children, local expertise in family-centered care should be drawn from state programs for Maternal and Child Health and for Children with Special Health Needs.

The data we collected on developmentally disabled children can be used to examine how the 1987 and 1989 Medicaid expansions would affect them. We found that roughly 7% of the children with autism and about 4% of those with severe mental retardation lacked insurance, as reported in Table 6.2. Young children appear to lack insurance slightly more often than youth. If states where half of all children lived were to use the 1987 Reconciliation Act to extend eligibility to 8-year-olds in poverty, that would barely affect disabled children and would reduce the uninsured proportion from about 6% to roughly 5.5%. By contrast, the 1989 amendments would extend Medicaid coverage to all the poor families in the Florida, Alabama, and Texas sites.

Four shortcomings diminish the blessings from expanding Medicaid to pay for children's services. One, the extreme variation among states in eligibility and services is unfair. Two, as a fee-for-service system, Medicaid has fragmentary cost containment mechanisms. Three, the review and financing system imposes a large record keeping burden on providers. Four, providers' fees allowable in many states are too low to attract new providers. Most of these problems are addressed by a proposal from a researcher at the Brookings Institution (Russell, 1989) to create a single, comprehensive health care system that serves all low income people.

Medicaid Increase of Home and Community Based Services

Medicaid waivers have been a flexible but complicated method for states to obtain permission from the Health Care Financing Administration (HCFA) to use federal funds for services provided outside of institutions. For people covered by a waiver, the state is free to provide specific services not included in the mandatory or optional state services and to decline to provide those services to others served by Medicaid. A balanced report on home care waivers in a sample of states has been made by the General Accounting Office (1989b). In recent years HCFA has preferred not to issue new waivers, but to encourage states to use their options flexibly.

The fundamental deficiency of family support services is addressed by the Medicaid Quality Services to the Mentally Retarded Amendments of 1988 sponsored by Representative Waxman, H.R. 5233. A succinct analysis prepared by the Congressional Budget Office (1988) estimates participation, services, and federal costs. The Waxman bill gives states the option of providing community habilitation services to individuals with mental retardation or related conditions. We believe that these services would be especially helpful for young adults who are no longer served by the special education system. Among the services covered are prevocational, adaptive living, educational, and supported employment. The individuals eligible for these services are those eligible for SSI, approximately 100,000 people, according to the Congressional Budget Office estimate, which also projects new enrollments at 42,000 by 1993.

Some of the major benefits of this bill to individuals who are severely retarded or autistic can be estimated from our data. Although all of the individuals in our study were categorically eligible for SSI, many were ineligible due to the amount of family income and assets. Only 40% of those living at home across the age span from birth to 24 received SSI benefits. A larger proportion of young adults at home, about 85%, received SSI benefits. The unserved young adults could receive SSI benefits under current regulations, while the unserved 72% of the families of children may need assistance that could come from change in regulations or from alternative sources.

State Medicaid programs have the option of covering several habilitative services particularly appropriate for seriously disabled children. The federal tally of states covering an optional service includes the state if it has authorized the service, no matter how many practical barriers limit or prevent its general use. Only 35 states covered physical therapy as of 1987, 25 covered occupational therapy, and 33 covered speech therapy (Health Care Financing Administration, 1988).

Expansion makes good sense because financial barriers should not be the criteria for determining whether or not a child will receive therapy. Good sense aside, if states have not chosen to cover these therapies during the first quarter century of the Medicaid program, the likelihood is low that they will in the present era of tight state budgets.

Medicaid Buy-ins

The Med-America bill that Senator John Chafee introduced in 1987 would guarantee insurance coverage by permitting people to buy Medicaid coverage if they lack private health insurance. A balanced assessment of the usefulness of Medicaid buy-ins for people with disabilities has been prepared by Bob Griss (1989). The premium would be adjusted to income and limited to 3% of adjusted gross income, and the services could exceed the usual Medicaid services by including those provided under the state's home and community based waivers. Concepts from this bill have been incorporated in other federal and state bills: Senator Kennedy's Minimum Health Benefits bill of 1989; the Massachusetts law of 1988, called CommonHealth; and feasibility studies in Wisconsin and Maine.

The Massachusetts plan for people with disabilities also solves the problem that private insurance usually does not cover preventive and home health services. Holders of private insurance are permitted to purchase supplemental coverage under the CommonHealth system of Medicaid buy-in. This wraparound package permits families to augment their private insurance by obtaining a full range of services from family planning to speech therapy.

Medicaid buy-ins are a clear example of filling the gaps. They have the advantage of not creating a new bureaucracy, unlike high-risk pools, but they carry the disadvantages of inequity among states and lack of effective cost containment.

Financial Support for Families

Support for unpaid caregivers comes in three forms: tax credits or deductions (for example, the federal government child and dependent care tax credit) direct payments to family members, as in the Michigan program of family support; and direct services to the unpaid provider, ranging from training to respite.

Tax breaks are always unobtrusive and often inequitable, but easy to administer. The longstanding federal tax exemption for a blind person leads to the question, why not for the deaf? Since the federal dependent care income tax credit applies to all children below age 15 and to disabled spouses, the obvious gaps are older disabled offspring and frail elderly relatives, but Congress has resisted expanding the scope. The amount of tax that the federal government forgoes in the child care tax credit—going largely to middle and upper income families—is larger than the amount spent on all Headstart and other day-care programs for disadvantaged children. This inequity promotes a two-tier system of child care.

Family financial support programs have the merit of giving families flexibility to meet their needs as they define them. An impressive example is the Michigan family support program for children under age 18. Families of children with severe or profound mental retardation, both physically and mentally impaired, or autistic are eligible for a subsidy of $225 per month as long as the family income is under $60,000. Since starting the program in 1984, Michigan now assists more than 3,000 families. The initial hope that a substantial number of families would bring their children home from residential placement proved to be false; only 60 have returned. The basic reason to mount such programs is that they help to relieve the burden on families.

Case Management through State Title V Programs

"Inappropriate medical care, contradictory advice for parents, duplication of painful and expensive procedures, premature alternation of management strategies, prolongation of symptoms, and unnecessary medical crises" may occur for lack of case management (Hobbs, Perrin, & Ireys, 1985, p.228). Case management opens up possibilities for enhancing the appropriateness of services in addition to addressing the inadequacy of insurance. The state Title V programs have had more than 50 years of financially supporting and directly providing services to medically complex children. Variation in the programs is described by a recent report from the General Accounting Office (1989a). The best of these programs have long been serving the families of special needs children (Healy, 1986).

The Future Directions Project of the National Maternal and Child Health Resource Center has provided an overview of CSHN services in the 50 states (Colton & Gittler, 1986), made an in-depth assessment of model programs in Florida, Iowa, Michigan, and Los Angeles (Colton & Gittler, 1986), provided an outline of issues and the text of relevant legislation (National Maternal and Child Health Resource Center, 1988), and conducted a national conference to communicate the findings (Colton & Gittler, 1987). The project identified three common elements in case management: an assessment of the child and the family; the development of a service plan; and continuing follow-up. An essential tool for parents performing case management for their own children is a guide to financing prepared by Julia Beckett (1989). Children with widely varying chronic conditions require care that is tailored to their individual needs and coordinated among various providers, as the Vanderbilt study has made clear (Hobbs et al., 1985).

For children who had case management, our study found that a substantial majority of parents judged that medical services had improved their children's lives. Appropriately, children with impaired ability to ambulate had case management three times more frequently than others. However, only about 20% of the children with autism had case management, as did about 40% of the children with severe mental retardation. By now, excellent case management programs are scattered across the country, such as REACH, serving children in rural Florida, and Minneapolis Children's Hospital, serving ventilator-assisted children. State CSHN programs are good vehicles to promote case management that supports family-centered care.

COORDINATED SYSTEMS FOR
PROVIDING CARE

Here we glance at two current modifications of the fragmented American system of providing health care: a national mandate for states to serve preschool children and a Utah program for all children. Their specific attention to children with special health care needs stands in contrast to the prevailing system, which neglects many needs of chronically disabled children. Both of them work within the constraints of the present fragmented financing system.

A national model is provided by the 1986 federal legislation for early intervention, P.L. 99-457, Education for the Handicapped Act Amendments (National Center for Clinical Infant Programs, 1989). A breakthrough, this legislation does not carve the child's needs into separate parcels called education and health. Rather, it looks at the whole child and the immediate family to ask what services are needed to prevent or reduce developmental delay in the child.

Each of the 50 states has designated a lead agency, usually the Department of Education or Health, to identify the children and provide diagnostic and habilitative services. Family service plans tailored to the needs of the infant and family will be coordinated through case management. The lead agency is responsible for assuring that the services are financed, including those not covered by current funding streams.

Medicaid, previously only a payer of last resort, was specifically required by P.L. 100-360 to become the first payer for children enrolled in Medicaid for any services that Medicaid covers under the state plan. The same broad perspective as in early intervention, which sees the needs of the whole child and family, should be adopted in shaping policies for the funding of services for developmentally disabled individuals.

Locating disabled children and making diagnoses are expensive services. The early intervention program of the Education for the Handicapped Act will identify the youngest ones who should be served. State special education programs have already identified school-age children and, through their rosters of school leavers, can trace young adults. The strengths of the 99-457 amendments to the Education for All Handicapped Children's Act are that they are equitable, provide an extensive range of services, and are family centered—three of the goals we seek in new programs. However, they are not administratively simple.

Utah has developed an impressive program of integrated services for children with special health needs that can serve as a model for other states. The state departments of education and health, the state Medicaid office, and the program of Services for Children with Special Health needs have integrated their data bases in order to serve special needs children. For example, the CSHN program provides case management and selects the professionals who provide appropriate therapies in the schools, funded by Medicaid. In sum, Utah has provided new services by coordinating the work of old agencies.

COORDINATED SYSTEMS FOR
FINANCING CARE

A number of serious proposals aim to expand both private and public coverage to reach the entire population. Senator Edward Kennedy's bill, already mentioned, is one. Another comes from the National Leadership Commission on Health Care (Newacheck, 1990). Instead of assessing each of these proposals, we will provide an overview of the most comprehensive one, the Pepper Commission recommendations, and an evaluation of the one tailored for children, from the American Academy of Pediatrics.

The Pepper Commission

In 1990 Congress is engaged in a major effort to provide health insurance to all Americans, having received in March from the bipartisan Pepper Commission on Comprehensive Health Care recommendations that address separately both health care an long-term care (Congress, 1990). The commission's forthcoming detailed report is anticipated to provide the basis for legislation that Senator Donald Riegle, chairman of the subcommittee on health of the Senate Finance Committee, intends to introduce.

The Commission uses both public and private sector approaches to tackle the three problems of lack of insurance, underinsurance, and catastrophic expenses. A key provision is that federal mandates will force businesses with more than 100 employees to either provide health insurance to all their employees and their nonworking dependents or pay a tax earmarked for the public plan that will cover everyone else. Small businesses would get short-term tax credits, and self-employed individuals could deduct their premiums. If small businesses as a group did nor insure at least 80% of their employees by the fifth year of the plan, then all such businesses would come under the requirements for large firms.

The public plan would initially cover children and pregnant women, but by year 5 it would include everyone not insured through employers. Although Medicaid would still exist, most of its functions would be assumed by the public plan, which would be financed and administered by the federal government, rather like Medicare. The Commission estimates the federal cost to be between $114 and $128 billion for the five year phase-in and $31 billion annually, thereafter. In aiming to reform the private insurance market, the commission flatly advocates abolishing the barrier that works such hardship on people with disabilities, the preexisting condition clause.

Catastrophic expenses for individuals and families would be eliminated through a variety of mandates to insurers. All policies would have to be based on community rating, premiums being identical for every group in the community. Maximum copayments would be set at 20%. Especially important for financially burdened families, annual out-of-pocket expenses could not exceed $3,000.

To solve problems of underinsurance, the federal government would mandate that insurers provide benefit packages that include prenatal care, well-child care, and other preventive services, for which no copayments would be required. Also covered would be hospital and physician services, diagnostic tests, and limited mental health services. The Pepper Commission's separate recommendations on long-term care itemize benefits that would be provided to individuals with severe disabilities of all ages: physical, occupational, and speech therapies, personal care services, respite and support counseling for family caregivers. These are the very services that our data show to be little used, or paid for exclusively by the family, or both.

Universal Health Care Access for Children and Pregnant Women

The comprehensive proposal of the American Academy of Pediatrics (AAP) is to create universal access to health care for children through age 21 and pregnant women through six weeks postpartum by creating universal insurance coverage (Lewin/ICF, 1989). Because the AAP plan would serve well the interests of children with disabilities and because it is politically feasible, we examined it at some length. Expense to the individuals covered would be limited, based on their ability to pay, and the minimum benefits package would provide a wide range of services, including free preventive care. The sponsorship of this proposal is impressive, the professional voice of American pediatricians. The approach would cover all children through two insurance systems, one that employers would be mandated to provide or else pay a 3.17% tax on wages, and one that would cover everyone else through 50 state funds.

The impressive benefits package composed of three "baskets" would be similar for all. One, the preventive care benefit basket, for which there would be no additional charges, includes routine medical office visits, immunizations, lab tests, prenatal and newborn care, and preventive dental care. Two, the major medical benefit basket contains all hospital and physician services, acute dental care, medical equipment and supplies, glasses, hearing aids, and prescription drugs. Copayments would be 20% for the privately insured and from 20% down on a sliding scale for individuals covered by the state plans. Three, the care-coordinated benefits basket contains all habilitative and therapeutic services, including mental health services, respite care, and recuperative stays in long-term care facilities. Here the copayments would be 30% for children covered through employers, and would vary by benefit for children covered by state funds.

The proposal requires the employer to pay 75% of the premium and sets low limits on the recipients' contributions to the state funds. Caps would prevent a family from paying more than 10% of income or $3,000 per year or $1,000 per child per year. The proposal presents preliminary revenue estimates at $24 billion from employers, about equally divided between enhanced insurance coverage and payroll taxes to support the state funds. The $35.6 billion in total revenues of the state funds would also include $15.3 billion from Medicaid and $7.5 billion from premiums.

This AAP proposal resolves all three shortcomings of our present system: lack of insurance, lack of coverage for needed services, and lack of protection against catastrophic payments. In sum, it would serve admirably the health care needs of the children in our study. The uninsured 7-8% of the autistic children and the uninsured 4-5% of the severely retarded children would receive coverage largely through private insurance, if the AAP estimates are correct that half of employers will expand coverage. Recall that three-quarters of the uninsured children in both disability categories had parents in full-time employment.

The benefits package was designed with intimate knowledge of the medical needs of children with chronic illnesses and disabilities as well as the common health care needs of all children. The inclusion of routine medical checkups in the preventive benefit basket could reduce the rate of failure for the nearly 30% of both autistic and severely retarded children under age 6 who did not have an annual physical exam.

The inclusion of dental examinations in preventive care should greatly assist in correcting the failure of about 40% of both autistic and severely retarded children to see a dentist within the previous 12 months (see Table 4.12.). Inclusion of dental services in the basket of major medical benefits would provide needed care. Recall from Tables 7.1 and 7.3 that the average annual expenditure for ambulatory dentistry for all autistic children was about $70 and for children with severe or profound retardation about $30 per capita. Private insurance and Medicaid combined paid on average no more than $25 and $10 respectively. If the AAP proposal requiring insurance to pay 80% were enacted, the family's dollars could cover more visits.

Examining each of the services in Table 7.1, we see that in the present system the families of children with autism paid out-of-pocket for more than 20% of the expenditures for physicians in private practice, outpatient visits, drugs, and supplies. The families of children with severe or profound retardation paid about 20% for each of these services, except supplies, where they paid half.

The third basket of benefits contains the many services that are so wanting for these children and their families. The current system provided case management for around 10% of the autistic children and 25% of the retarded children, physical or occupational therapy for about one quarter of the children who could benefit, and respite for less than 10% of the families. The AAP proposal takes an impressively broad view of what is a health care service.

The stop-loss provisions for family expenditures would clearly help financially burdened families such as those in our study. We performed a special data analysis to estimate the number of families whose spending exceeded the AAP limits. Out-of-pocket spending on all health and care services required due to the child's disability, as defined in Table 8.1, exceeded $1,000 per child for about one-third of the autistic children and about 40% of the severely retarded children. If family medical spending is narrowly defined as in Table 8.2, over 10% of the families with autistic children and almost 25% of the families of children with severe retardation would use this protection.

In applying the AAP stop-loss provisions regarding spending for all children in the family, we conservatively estimated that our families spent $200 per child for nondisabled siblings. In both individual and family computations, we used the medical consumer price index to adjust the 1985-86 data to 1990 prices. We found that about 10% of the families of autistic children spent more than 10% of their income if broad services were considered, and a mere 2% spent more using the narrow definition of services. An additional 2% of the families with incomes over $30,000 would be protected against spending more than $3,000 for total services.

Families with children who have severe or profound retardation would benefit much more from the 10% limit because, on average, their out-of-pocket expenses are higher and their incomes lower. The 10% limit would protect about 30% of the families using a broad definition of services and about 10% using a narrow definition. Separately, the $3,000 limit would protect over 15% using the broad definition of health care services and over 10% using the narrow definition.

The AAP proposal meets admirably the first three of the seven goals proposed at the outset of the chapter: preventive focus, universal coverage of children, and a broad definition of health care. We judge it to be highly equitable. However, its strength in targeting children results in weakness in meeting the criterion of being family centered, as the parents' health is neglected. Respite is the one family service now included in the proposal, but mental health services for family members are not.

Another problem with the proposal is that it does not address the transition to adulthood, and its most serious shortcoming is its administrative complexity. By creating 50 state funds for children, it adds to the existing complexity because Medicaid and state high-risk pools remain necessary for noninsured adults. A clear advantage of the plan is that it should prove highly cost-effective in the long run, due to its restriction to children and its emphasis on free preventive services from family planning to dental care.

INTEGRATED SYSTEMS
FOR FINANCING AND
DELIVERING CARE

After a decade of public discussion of the ills of the American health care system, 67% of Americans now favor a government financed national health plan (Blendon & Donelan, 1989). Interest is growing in how the Canadian national health system provides quality service while holding down medicine's share of the GNP. An editorial in *The New England Journal of Medicine* declared that the time has come for universal health insurance (Relman, 1989). One of the two proposals it reviewed, by an advocacy group called Physicians for A National Health Program, calls for a single, comprehensive public insurance program that would cover everyone, pay hospitals an annual sum to cover all operating expenses, and pay physicians in any of three ways: as employees of hospitals, through a standard fee-for-service, or on a per capita basis.

Legislation introduced by Representative Ronald Dellums (H.R. 2402, 100th Congress) goes further in calling for a national health service to employ physicians. The value of these and other far-reaching legislative proposals to the health care of children is ably summarized by Newacheck (1990). Although politically less feasible in the short run, a single national system that pays for health care through general tax revenues could prove to be the best means to meet the health care needs of children with developmental disabilities and of all Americans.

CONCLUSIONS

We return to the seven goals of reform set out at the opening of this chapter as we summarize policy options recently adopted or proposed by Congress and state legislatures. As a whole, most attention is addressed to managing the risk of disability through providing health insurance for all.

Primary prevention of developmental disabilities will be enhanced through the 1989 mandate that states provide Medicaid coverage to pregnant women and infants up to 133% of poverty. Evaluation of the effects of this legislation will probably prove it cost-effective in prevention of mental retardation due to maternal substance abuse, poor nutrition, and other environmental risks.

Within the disability field, family planning receives little attention. Genetic counseling can, for many syndromes, inform parents of their risk of having a developmentally disabled child, but national policy does little to promote genetic screening and counseling. Failure to address these issues is illustrated by the 200-page summary of legislation affecting persons with disabilities produced by the Office of Special Education (1988) and Braddock's 1987 monograph on federal policies toward mental retardation and developmental disabilities. Both books are silent on reproductive issues.

In both private and public sector strategies a major goal is to end the national embarrassment presented by the fact that 34 million are uninsured. The cost of private sector strategies will not be shared equitably unless Congress amends ERISA to set employer mandates directly or to permit states to regulate self-insured corporations. The attractiveness of private sector strategies is that they will not require new taxes, but public sector strategies have the advantages of being more comprehensive and administratively simpler.

The broad range of services typically required by children with disabilities is more comprehensively covered by Medicaid and CSHN programs than by private insurance, which focuses on physicians and hospitals. A wrap-around policy, such as the Massachusetts CommonHealth program, permits parents to supplement their private insurance by purchasing public coverage for whatever their private insurance policy omits, from dentistry to personal care services.

Family centered approaches are in their infancy. The many movements to promote individual rights for blacks, women, gays, and people with disabilities have obscured the fact that people are not isolated individuals; indeed the great majority live with their families, and those who live apart from family typically have family members and friends who mean a great deal to them. Children, in particular, need families. The average person is not independent, but shares an interdependence. Current focus on achieving independence for disabled people neglects the members of their households, people who carry a burden beyond the ones most people bear. If policy addressed the immediate family as the unit that needs services due to a member's disability, respite services would be common, rather than the rarity we found them to be.

The transition to adult services is not addressed coherently by the health care system. We deliberately expanded the scope of our study to age 24 because we were concerned about the gap in financing as children come of age. In fact, for children who are so severely disabled that they are unable to hold gainful employment, financing through SSI and, in most states, concomitant access to Medicaid, can begin at age 18. What is striking is the chasm in services that the youth faces upon leaving school.

Not one of the policy initiatives reviewed is administratively simple. If solution of these problems continues to follow models from the past, the picture will become more complicated. Stepping outside of the health field to look at other social services, we see an enduring American distaste for uniform national solutions. Whether the topic is education or police protection or welfare, Americans enjoy very complicated and diverse patterns of service provision. Because Medicaid is a joint federal-state program, complexities and inequities arise between the generous and less generous states. If only some state governments provide insurance coverage for the uninsured, inequality and complexity will increase. In sum, it seems that in the near future we will not avoid increasing the complexity found in the financing of health care.

A complex system makes it harder to contain costs, and cost containment is the watchword today. Accordingly, throughout this study, we have documented great variation in the utilization of health services and in expenditure patterns that cannot be accounted for strictly by the physical condition of the child. Further analysis of our data can tease out the contributions to cost containment of case management, the site of service delivery, the services of a pediatrician as primary physician, and the type of third party payer.

The many strategies for private and public sector reform each have their price tags for the federal treasury, calculated by the Congressional Budget Office and by the Administration. They each have their private cost and their social cost. With all the plans afloat to provide universal insurance coverage, the results of the RAND experiment must be taken seriously: that having insurance coverage increases health care expenditures. Health maintenance organizations and other capitation plans work well for the general population in providing comprehensive services for modest expenditures, but early research shows that they serve children with developmental disabilities less well than children with chronic medical conditions (Karlson et al., 1990).

The argument has not been advanced for years that Americans are spending too little on health. There is consensus that the health care share of the national economy is sufficient but that present distribution of health care is inequitable. We believe that the major inequities found in the care of children with chronic conditions should have high priority on the agenda for reform.

Chapter 11

Summary and Conclusions

The 1985-86 data from 308 children and young adults under age 25 with autism and from 326 with severe or profound mental retardation can be compared to national data from the 1980 MNCUES and the 1987 NMES because the methods are similar. These data provide detailed answers to the questions, what health care services are used? what are the expenses? Who pays them? Until now, the absence of comprehensive national data had hindered the development of new approaches to financing the care of children with serious, lifelong conditions.

These data permit policymakers to take into account the needs and expenditures for severely developmentally disabled children when reforming the health care financing system. None of the children or young adults had expenditures in excess of $50,000, and very few reached the upper $20,000s.

For children with autism the average annual health care expenditure was about $1,000 and about $1,700 for young adults, compared to the $414 average for all American children. They received an average of four physician visits annually, slightly above the U.S. average for children. Their hospitalization rate was twice the average for children. Hospitalization accounted for one-third the health care expenditures among children with autism, but for two-thirds among young adults.

For children and young adults with severe retardation the average expenditure on health care was about $4,000, due to the physical impairments in two thirds of the children. They averaged about 12 physician visits annually, falling to 8 among young adults. Children were hospitalized about eight times the national rate, and young adults about twice. Among severely retarded children and young adults living at home, hospitalization accounted for over half the health care expenses, but for only one third for those in residential placement. Unfortunately, preventive and habilitative services were but a tiny fraction of health care expenditures and were demonstrably underutilized. Only 60% of these children had routine dental examinations within the last 12 months, a worse record than the average child. For the individuals whose primary physicians judged that they would benefit from physical or speech therapy, less than one quarter were receiving them.

Care for seriously, chronically disabled children places great burdens on immediate family members. Only 20% of the severely retarded youngsters from age 10 to 24 could be left alone at home, even for a few minutes, and only

30% of the autistic ones. These developmental disabilities create needs for personal care and family support that traditionally have not been considered health services. Overnight respite was used by less than 10% of the families with an autistic child and by less than 15% of the families with a child who had severe or profound retardation. For autistic children and young adults, family out-of-pocket expenses for child care, programs, respite, travel for medical care, home and car modification, and damage replacement equal the amount for traditional health care.

Inequities abound in the financing of health care. Almost 20% of the parents of children with severe or profound retardation, and 10% of the parents of autistic children had experienced refusals or limitations in the health insurance they could buy for their child. In both disability groups, about 15% of those with private insurance had policies that specifically excluded coverage for some of the child's care.

The overall picture among autistic children and young adults is that about 20% had coverage from both private insurance and public programs, about 50% had strictly private coverage, about 25% had only public coverage, leaving about 7% uninsured. Among individuals with severe retardation, about 30% had both, about 25% had private insurance only, about 40% had public only, and about 4% were uninsured. As a consequence, the percentage of uninsured children who did not visit a physician during 12 months was three times higher than for insured children. Black children in both disability groups and across the age span used physician services at about half the rate of white children.

For autistic children, the average out-of-pocket expenses for health and personal care was almost $1,000, about 3% of family income, but a very few families, about 2%, had expenses greater than 15% of their income. Families with a child who has severe or profound retardation typically spent almost $2,000 out-of-pocket, an average of 7% of their income, but as many as 10% spent over 15% of their total income. Medical debts over $2,000 burdened 1% of the families with autistic children and 5% of the families with children who have severe or profound retardation.

New policies to correct these inequities will be relatively inexpensive because children with severe developmental disabilities are rare, most of them are already covered by private insurance or public programs, and the average expense per child is modest. We welcome the use of this study by families, advocates, providers, payers, and policymakers in their efforts to assist all children in the United States to have a decent start in life.

References

Aday, L. A., Wegener, D. H., Andersen, R. M., and Aitken, M. J. (1989). Data watch: Home care for ventilator-assisted children. *Health Affairs, 8,* Summer, 102-110.

Aledort, L. M., & Diaz, M. (1982). The cost of care for hemophiliacs. In M. W. Hilgartner (Ed.), *Hemophilia in the child and the adult* (pp. 187-193). New York: Masson.

Allen, D. A. (1988). Autistic spectrum disorders: Clinical presentation in preschool children. *Journal of Child Neurology, 3* (Supplement), S48-S49.

American Academy of Pediatrics. (1977). *Standards of Child Health Care* (3rd ed.). Evanston, IL: Author.

Andersen, R., Lion, J., & Anderson, O. (1976). *Two decades of health services: Social survey trends in use and expenditure.* Cambridge, MA: Ballinger.

Anderson, O. (1985). *Health services in the United States.* Ann Arbor, MI: Health Administration Press.

Austin, J. (1984). Sounding board: Child health care financing and competition. *New England Journal of Medicine, 75,* 1117-1120.

Beckett, J. (1989). *Health care financing: A guide for families.* Iowa City, IA: University of Iowa, National Maternal and Child Resource Center.

Blendon, R., & Donelan, K. (1989). The 1988 election: How important was health? *Health Affairs, 8* (3), 7-15.

Blue Cross and Blue Shield, Office of Government Relations. (1990). *State mandated coverages.* Washington, DC: Author.

Braddock, D. (1987). *Federal policy toward mental retardation and developmental disabilities.* Baltimore: Paul H. Brookes.

Bradley, V. M., & Agosta, J. M. (1985). *Family care for persons with developmental disabilities: A growing commitment.* Boston: Human Services Research Institute.

Brewer, G. D., & deLeon, P. (1983). *The foundations of policy analysis.* Homewood, IL: The Dorsey Press.

Brewer, G. D., & Kakalik, J. S. (1979). *Handicapped children: Strategies for improving services.* New York: McGraw-Hill.

Bryson, S. D., Clark, B. S., & Smith, I. M. (1987). First report of a Canadian epidemiological study of autistic syndromes. *Journal of Child Psychology & Psychiatry, 29,* 433-445.

Budetti, P. P., Butler, J. A., & McManus, M. A. (1982). Federal health program reforms: Implications for child health care. *Milbank Memorial Fund Quarterly, 60,* 155-181.

Bureau of the Census. (1983a). *Census of population and housing, 1980: Summary tape file STF3 technical documentation.* Washington, DC: United States Department of Commerce.

Bureau of the Census. (1983b). *County and city data book, 1983.* Washington, DC: U.S. Government Printing Office.

Bureau of the Census. (1983c). *State and metropolitan area databook, 1983.* Washington, DC: U.S. Government Printing Office.

Bureau of the Census. (1987a). *Current population report p-20: Maternal status and living arrangements, March 1986.* Washington, DC: U.S. Government Printing Office.

Bureau of the Census. (1987b). *Money income of households, families, and persons in the United States.* Washington, DC: U.S. Government Printing Office.

Bureau of Labor Statistics. (1987). Employee benefits in medium and large firms, 1986 (Bulletin 2281). Washington, DC: U.S. Government Printing Office.

Burr, B. H., Guyer, B., Todres, I. D., Abrahams, B., & Chiodo, T.(1983). Home care for children on respirators. *New England Journal of Medicine, 309,* 1319-1323.

Butler, J. A., Budetti, P. P., McManus, M. A., Stenmark, M. S., & Newacheck, P. A. (1985). Health care expenditures for children with chronic disabilities. In N. Hobbs & J. M. Perrin (Eds.), *Issues in the care of children with chronic illness: A sourcebook on problems, services and policies* (pp. 827-863). San Francisco: Jossey-Bass.

Butler, J. A., Singer, J. D., Palfrey, J. S., & Walker, D. K. (1987). Health insurance coverage and physician use among children with disabilities: Findings from probability samples in five metropolitan areas. *Pediatrics, 79,* 89-98.

Callahan, J., Jr., Plough, A. L., & Wisensale, S. (1981). *Long term care of children.* Unpublished paper, University Health Policy Consortium, Waltham, MA.

Children's Defense Fund. (1989). *A vision for America's future, an agenda for the 1990s: A children's defense budget.* Washington, DC: Author.

Cohodes, D. R. (1986). America: The home of the free, the land of the uninsured. *Inquiry, 23,* 227-235.

Colton, M., & Gittler, J. (1986). *The Title V state programs and the provision of case management services for children with special health care needs* (grant # MCJ-193790-01). Washington, DC: Division of Maternal and Child Health.

Colton, M., & Gittler, J. (eds.) (1987). *Community-based case management programs for children with special health care needs* (grant #MCJ-193790-01). Washington, DC: Division of Maternal and Child Health.

Congressional Budget Office. (1988). Estimated costs and provisions of H. R. 3454 and H. R. 5233. Staff Working Paper, Congress of the United States.

Davidson, S. M. (1979). The status of aid to the medically needy. *Social Science Review, 92,* March, 92-105.

Davidson, S. M., Friedman, B. S., & Mannheim, L. (1985). *State Medicaid policies: Variations, trends, and outcomes, 1978-1982.* Unpublished paper. Center for Health Services and Policy Research, Northwestern University: Evanston, IL.

DeMyer, M., Hingtgen, J. N., & Jackson, R. K. (1981). Infantile autism reviewed: A decade of research. *Schizophrenia Bulletin, 7,* 388-451.

Division of Maternal and Child Health Services. (1984). Report of workshop on financing health care for handicapped children, Vienna, VA.

Donn, S. (1982). Cost effectiveness of home management of bronchopulmonary dysplasia. *Pediatrics, 70,* 330-331.

Eyster, M. E., Lewis, J. H., Shapiro, S. S., Gill, F., Kajani, M., Prager, D., Djerassi, I., Rice, S., Lusch, C., & Keller, A. (1980). The Pennsylvania hemophilia program, 1973-1978. *American Journal of Hematology, 9,* 277-286.

Fox, H. B., & Neiswander, L. (1989). *The financing and delivery of community care services to the elderly: Lessons learned for disabled children.* Washington, DC: The Bureau of Maternal and Child Health, Department of Health and Human Services.

Freedman, S. A., Klepper, B. R., Duncan, R. P., & Bell, S. P.(1988). Coverage of the uninsured and underinsured. *The New England Journal of Medicine, 318,* 843-847.

General Accounting Office. (1989a). *Health care: Children's medical services programs in 10 states.* Report to the Chairman, Committee on Finance, U.S. Senate (GAO/HRD-89-81).

General Accounting Office. (1989b). *Health care: Nine states' experience with home care waivers.* Report to the Chairman, Committee on Finance, U.S. Senate (GAO/HRD-89-95).

Ginzburg, E. (Ed.). (1985). *The U.S. health care system: A look to the 1990s.* Lanham, MD: Rowman and Allenheld.

Griss, B. (1988). *Access to Health Care, 1,* (1, 2). (Oakland, CA: World Disability Institute, 510 Sixteenth St., Oakland, CA 94612).

Griss, B. (1989). *Access to Health Care, 1,* (3, 4).

Guyot, D., & Birenbaum, A. (1986a, May). *You'll find the kids in school.* Paper presented at the annual meeting of the American Association for Public Opinion Research, St. Petersburg, FL.

Guyot, D., & Birenbaum, A. (1986b, May). *Rare and costly: Concepts underlying policy research on the financing of health care for children who are chronically and severely disabled.* Paper presented at the Center for Health Administration Studies, The University of Chicago.

Hansen, H., Belmont, L., & Stein, Z. (1980). Epidemiology. In J. Wortis (Ed.), *Mental retardation and developmental disabilities: An annual review* (pp.21-54). New York: Brunner/Mazel Inc.

Health and Human Services. (1990). *HHS News,* May 3, 1990.

Health Care Financing Administration, Office of the Actuary.(1988a). National health expenditures, 1986-2000. *Health Care Financing Review, 8,* 4, 34.

Health Care Financing Administration. (1988b). *Medical services by state.* Washington, DC: Author.

Healy, A., Keesee, P. D., &. Smith, B. S. (1986). *Early services for children with special needs: Transactions for family support.* Iowa City: Division of Developmental Disabilities, University of Iowa Hospital School.

Hobbs, N., Perrin, J. M., & Ireys, H. T. (1985). *Chronically ill children and their families.* San Francisco: Jossey-Bass.

Ireys, H. T. & Eichler, R. J. (1988). *Correlates of variation among state programs for children with special health care needs: Report of survey and six case studies.* Rockville, MD: Division of The Maternal and Child Health and Crippled Children's Services Research Grants Program.

Kalton, G. (1983). *Compensating for missing survey data.* Ann Arbor: The University of Michigan, Survey Research Center, Institute for Social Research.

Karlson, T. A., Sumi, M. D., & Braucht, S. A. (1990). *The impact of health maintenance organizations on accessibility, satisfaction and cost of health care for children with special needs.* Madison, WI: Center for Health Systems Research and Analysis and Center for Public Representation.

Kasper, J. D. (1986). *Perspectives on health care: United States, 1980.* National Medical Care Expenditure Survey, Series B, Descriptive Report #14. Washington, DC: Health Care Financing Administration.

Kaufman, J., & Lichenstein, K. (1986). *The family as care manager: Home care coordination for medically fragile children.* Washington, DC: Georgetown University Child Development Center.

Kearney, K. A., Hopkins, R. H., Mauss, A. L., & Weistiet (1983). Sample bias resulting from a requirement for written parental consent. *Public Opinion Quarterly, 47,* 96-111.

Kiely, M. (1987). The prevalence of mental retardation. *Epidemiologic Review, 9,* 194-218.

Kiernan, W. E., and Bruininks, R. H. (1986). Demographic characteristics, in W. E. Kiernan and J. A. Stark, eds. *Pathways to employment for adults with developmental disabilities.* Baltimore, MD: Paul H. Brookes.

Kimmich, M. H. (1985). *America's children: Who cares? Growing needs and declining assistance in the Reagan era.* Washington, DC: Urban Institute Press.

Kohrman, A. (1989). Facing the financing of care. In R. K. Stein (Ed.), *Caring for children with chronic diseases* (pp.268-281). New York: Springer.

Krischer, J. P., & Cook, B. A. (1985). State and federal expenditures on Medicaid eligible chronically ill children in rural Florida. *Journal of Chronic Diseases, 38,* 951-956.

Lakin, K. C., Jaskulski, T. M., Hill, E. K., Bruininks, R. H., Menke, J. M., White, C. C., & Wright, E. A. (1989). *Medicaid services for persons with mental retardation and related conditions* (Project Report 27, May 1989). Minneapolis: University of Minnesota, Institute on Community Integration.

Lansky, S. B., Cirns, N., Clark, G., Lowman, J., Miller, C., & Treeworthy, R. (1979). Childhood cancer: Nonmedical costs of the illness. *Cancer, 43,* 403-408.

Letsch, S. W., Levit, K. R., and Waldo, D. R. (1988). National Health Expenditures, 1987. *Health Care Financing Review, 10* (2), 109-129.

Levine, P. H. (1974). Efficacy of self-therapy in hemophilia. *New England Journal of Medicine, 291,* 1381-1384.

Levine, P. H. (1975). Delivery of health care in hemophilia. *Annals of the New York Academy of Sciences, 240,* 201-207.

Lewin/ICF (1989). *American Academy of Pediatrics proposal for universal access to health care for children and pregnant women.* Chicago: American Academy of Pediatrics.

Lewin, M. E. (Ed.) (1985). *The health policy agenda: Some critical questions.* Washington, DC: American Enterprise Institute for Public Research.

Linney, D. R., & Lazarson, J. (1979). Hemophilia: Cost considerations for prescribing therapeutic materials. *Transfusion, 19,* 57-59.

Majure, G. (1981). Tennessee hemophilia program. *Journal of the Tennessee Medical Association, 74,* 747-748.

Martinson, I. M., Armstrong, G. D., Geis, D. P., Anglim, M. A., Gronseth, E. C., MacInnis, H, Kersey, J. H., & Nesbit, M. E., Jr. (1979). Home care for children dying with cancer. *Pediatrics, 62,* 1, 106-113.

McCollum, A. T. (1971). Cystic fibrosis: Economic impact upon the family. *American Journal of Public Health, 61,* 1335-1340.

McFarlane, D. (1982). *Cost, utilization and percent of services covered by various sources, 1971-1974: Totals for myelomeningoceles.* As quoted in Butler et al., Health Care Expenditures for Children with Chronic Disabilities. Unpublished paper, Vanderbilt project, Public Policies Affecting Chronically Ill Children and their Families. Nashville, TN: Vanderbilt University.

McLaughlin, J. F., & Shurtleff, D. B. (1978). Management of the newborn with myelodysplasia. *Clinical Pediatrics, 18,* 463-476.

McManus, M. A., Melus, S. E., Norton, C. H., & Brauer, M. F. (1986). *Guide to national data on maternal and child health, with special emphasis on financing services for chronically ill children.* Washington, DC: Division of Maternal and Child Health, Public Health Service.

Meyers, R. D., Adams, W., Dardick, K., Reinisch, J., von Reyn, F., Renna, T., & McIntyre, O. R. (1972). The social and economic impact of hemophilia—A survey of 70 cases in Vermont and New Hampshire. *American Journal of Public Health, 62,* 530-535.

Moldow, D. G., Armstrong, G. D., Henry, W. F., & Martinson, I. M. (1982). The cost of home care for dying children. *Medical Care, 20,* 1154-1160.

National Academy of Sciences, Institute of Medicine, Division of Mental Health and Behavioral Medicine. (1989). *Research on children and adolescents with mental, behavioral, and developmental disorders: Mobilizing a national initiative.* Washington, DC: National Academy Press.

National Center for Clinical Infant Programs. (1989). *The intent and spirit of P.L. 99-457.* Washington, DC: Author.

National Center for Health Services Research. (1980). Health care surveys using diaries. *NCHSR Research Report Series.* Hyattsville, MD: Public Health Service.

National Center for Health Services Research. (1981). NMCES household interview instruments. Instruments and Procedures 1. *National health care expenditures study.* Washington, DC: Public Health Service.

National Center for Health Services Research. (1987). *National medical expenditure survey technical working documents.* Unpublished paper. Public Health Service: Rockville, MD.

National Center for Health Services Research. (1989). *A profile of uninsured Americans, 1989.* Rockville, MD: Public Health Service.

National Center for Health Statistics. (1975). Family out-of-pocket health expenses. *Vital and Health Statistics,* Series 10, Number 127. Washington, DC: Public Health Service.

National Center for Health Statistics. (1983). *Procedures and questionnaires of the National Medical Care Utilization and Expenditure Survey.* Series A, Methodological Report No. 1. Washington, DC: Public Health Service.

National Center for Health Statistics. (1985). *High and low volume users of health services, United States, 1980.* Series C, Analytic Report No. 2. Washington, DC: Public Health Service.

National Center for Health Statistics. (1986). *Cost of illness: United States, 1980.* Series C, Analytic Report No. 3. Washington, DC: Public Health Service.

National Center for Health Statistics. (1987a). *Family out-of-pocket expenditures for health care, 1980.* National Medical Care Utilization and Expenditure Survey. Series B, Descriptive Report No. 11. DHHS Pub. No 87-20211. Washington, DC: Public Health Service.

National Center for Health Statistics. (1987b). *Current estimates from the National Health Interview Survey, 1986.* Series 10, No. 164. Washington, DC: Public Health Service.

National Hemophilia Foundation, Cumberland Chapter. (1978). *A comprehensive survey of the hemophilia and related hemorrhagic disordered population.* Unpublished paper.

National Maternal and Child Health Resource Center. (1988, June). *Case management for children with special health care needs: children with special health care needs continuing education.* Introductory Institute, Columbus, OH.

Newacheck, P. W. (1990, February). *Improving access to care for expectant mothers and young children.* A paper presented at the Cornell Health Policy Conference VI, Improving the Life Chances of Children at Risk, New York, NY.

Newacheck, P. W., & Butler, L. H. (1983). Patterns of physician use among low income, chronically ill persons. *Medical Care, 21,* 981-989.

Newacheck, P. W., & Halfon, N. (1986). Access to ambulatory care services for economically disadvantaged children. *Pediatrics, 78,* 813-819.

Office of Disease Prevention and Health Promotion. (1986). *The 1990 health objectives for the nation: A midcourse review.* Washington, DC: Public Health Service.

Office of Special Education and Rehabilitative Services Clearinghouse on the Handicapped. (1985). *Summary of existing legislation affecting persons with disabilities.* Washington, DC: U.S. Government Printing Office.

Office of Technology Assessment. (1988). *Healthy children: Investing in the future.* Washington, DC: U.S. Government Printing Office.

Palfrey, J. S., Singer, J. D., Raphael, E. S., and Walker, D. K. (1990). Providing therapeutic services to children in special educational placements: An analysis of the related services provisions of Public Law 94-142 in five urban school districts. *Pediatrics, 85*, 518-525.

Perrin, J. M. (1986). Changing patterns of hospitalization for children requiring surgery. *Pediatrics, 77*, 587-592.

Pinney, M. A., & Cotton, E. K. (1976). Home management of bronchopulmonary dysplasia. *Pediatrics, 58*, 856-859.

President's Commission for the Study of Ethical Problems in Medicine and Biomedical and Behavioral Research. (1983). *Summing up: Final report.* Washington, DC: U.S. Government Printing Office.

Public Health Service. (1976). The uses of a multiple entry diary in a panel study on health care expenditure. Reprinted from the Proceedings of 1976 Social Statistics Section of the American Statistical Association. Washington, DC: Author.

Public Health Service. (1980). *Perspectives on health care: United States, 1980. National Medical Care Utilization and Expenditure Survey, Series B,* Descriptive Report No. 14. Washington, DC: Author.

Public Health Service. (1981). *Better health for our children: A national strategy.* (The Report of the Select Panel for the Promotion of Child Health to the U.S. Congress and the Secretary of Health and Human Services) Washington, DC: Department of Health and Human Services.

Public Health Service. (1987). *Children with special health care needs.* (Surgeon General's Report, Campaign '87. Commitment to Family Centered Coordinated Care for Children with Special Health Care Needs.) Washington, DC: Department of Health and Human Services.

Relman, A. S. (1989). Universal health insurance: Its time has come. *The New England Journal of Medicine, 320,* 2, 117-118.

Richardson, S. A. (1984). Institutionalization and deinstitutionalization of children with mental retardation. In H. Stevenson & A. Siegel (Eds.), *Child Development Research and Social Policy* (pp. 318-362). Chicago: University of Chicago Press.

Rivlin, A. M., & Wiener J. M. (1988). *Caring for the disabled elderly: Who will pay?* Washington, DC: The Brookings Institution.

Rossiter, L. F., & Wilensky, G. R. (1982). *Out-of-pocket expenditures for personal health services.* Data Preview 13. Washington, DC: National Center for Health Services Research.

Russell, L. B. (1989). A health care system for all the poor. *The Brookings Review, 7* (3), 13-20.

Savas, E. S. (1987). *Privatization: The key to better government.* Chatham, NJ: Chatham House.

Schorr, L. B., & Schorr, D. (1988). *Within our Reach.* New York: Anchor Books.

Schramm, C. J. (Ed.). (1987). *Health care and its costs.* New York: W. W. Norton.

Shelton, T. L., Jeppson, E. S., & Johnson, B. H. (1987). *Family-centered care for children with special health care needs.* Washington, DC: Association for the Care of Children's Health.

Singer, J. D., Butler, J. A., & Palfrey, J. S. (1986). Health care access and use among handicapped students in five public school systems. *Medical Care, 24,* 1-13.

Smith, P. S., Keyes, N. C., & Forman, E. N. (1982). Socioeconomic evaluation of a state-funded comprehensive hemophilia-care program. *The New England Journal of Medicine, 306,* 575-579.

Smyth-Staruch, K., Breslau, N., Weitzman, M., & Gortmaker, S.(1984). Use of health services by chronically ill and disabled children. *Medical Care, 22,* 310-328.

Southern California Kaiser Permanente Medical Care Program. (1987, March). Regional pilot project: *Home care for hospitalized ventilator-dependent patients: 1985-1987.* Paper presented to the Health Care Finance Administration Task Force, Torrance, CA.

Starfield, B. H., & Dutton, D. (1985). Care, costs and health: Reactions to and reinterpretation of the Rand findings. *Pediatrics, 76,* 614-621.

Starfield, B. H., Katz, H., Gabriel, I., Livingston, G., Benson, P., Hankin, J., Horn, S., & Steinwachs, D. (1984). Morbidity in childhood: A longitudinal view. *The New England Journal 'of Medicine, 310,* (13), 824-829.

Starr, P. (1982). *The social transformation of American medicine.* New York: Basic Books.

Stein, R. K. (Ed.), (1989). *Caring for children with chronic illness: Issues and strategies.* New York: Springer.

Stein, Z. A., & Susser, M. (1986). Mental retardation. In J. M. Last (Ed.), *Public health and preventative medicine,* 12th Ed. (pp. 1313-1326). Norwalk, CT: Appleton, Century-Crofts.

Strawczynski, H., Stachewitsch, A., Morgenstern, G., & Shaw, M. E. (1973). Delivery of care to hemophiliac children: Home care versus hospitalization. *Pediatrics, 51,* 986-991.

Strayer, F., Kisker, T., & Fethke, C. (1980). Cost-effectiveness of a shared-management delivery system for the care of children with cancer. *Pediatrics, 66,* 907-911.

Sultz, H. A., Schlesinger, E. R., Mosher, W. E., & Feldman, J. G. (1972). *Long-term childhood illness.* Pittsburgh: University of Pittsburgh Press.

Survey Research Laboratory. (1982). *Household network surveys of cancer care costs: A research pilot study.* Vol. 1 and Vol. 2. Champaign: University of Illinois.

Trippler, A. K. (1987). *Comprehensive health insurance for high-risk individuals: A state-by-state analysis.* Minneapolis: Communicating for Agriculture, Inc.

Valdez, R. B., Leibowitz, A., Ware, J. E., Jr., Duan, N., Goldberg, G. A., Keeler, E. B., Lohr, K. N., Manning, W. G., Jr., Rogers, W. H., Camp, P., Sherboune, C. A., Brook, R. H., & Newhouse, J. P. (1986). Health insurance, medical care and children's health. *Pediatrics, 77,* 124-128.

Vance, V. J., & Taylor, W. F. (1971). The financial cost of chronic childhood asthma. *Annals of Allergy, 29,* 455-460.

Waldo, D. R., Sonnefeld, S. T., McKusick, D. R., and Arnett, R. H., III, (1989). Health care expenditures by group. *Health Care Financing Review, 10,* 4, 111-120.

Walker, D. K., & Richmond, J. B. (Eds.). (1984). *Monitoring child health in the United States: Selected issues and policies.* Cambridge, MA: Harvard University Press.

Wing, L., & Gould, J. (1979). Severe impairments of social interaction and associated abnormalities in children: Epidemiology and classification. *Journal of Autism and Developmental Disorders, 9,* 11-29.

About the Authors

Arnold Birenbaum, Ph.D.

Currently Visiting Professor of Health Care Administration at Baruch College, City University of New York, Arnold Birenbaum specializes in health care policy research, including the social consequences of financing, responses to disability, and the development of new health care professions.

The author and/or editor of 10 scholarly books, Birenbaum's most recent efforts include *In the Shadow of Medicine: Remaking the Division of Labor in Health Care* (1990) and *Community Services for the Mentally Retarded* (1985), co-authored with Herbert J. Cohen.

He has published articles in the *American Journal on Mental Retardation, Mental Retardation, Social Science and Medicine, The Journal of Health and Social Behavior,* and many other journals.

Birenbaum conducted one of the first prospective studies and published one of the first monographs on deinstitutionalization in the United States. He holds a doctorate from Columbia University and is a Professor of Sociology at St. John's University/New York.

Dorothy Guyot, Ph.D.

Dorothy Guyot has served as Research Director of the Children's Evaluation and Rehabilitation Center of Albert Einstein College of Medicine since 1984. A political scientist, she received her bachelor's degree from the University of Chicago and her doctorate from Yale in 1966.

She has taught social science research methods, as a mode of clear thinking, to students at Columbia, Barnard, John Jay College of Criminal Justice, and Rutgers University. Her research inquires into the design of political and social institutions.

Guyot has worked as Assistant Director of Nursing for Clinical Research at Mount Sinai Medical Center, served as consultant on research design to the Nursing Department of Ramathibodi Hospital in Bangkok, and lectured at the ASEAN Primary Health Training Centre, Bangkok.

At Einstein she also directed the research on a three-year project to prevent child neglect among intellectually limited mothers and served on the advisory committee of the Preventive Intervention Research Center.

She has given presentations at the Brookings Institution conference on long-term care and the American Pediatric Society meetings and has served on the Congressional Office of Technology Assessment workshop on technologically dependent children.

Recently, she joined the faculty of St. John's College in Annapolis, MD to resume liberal arts teaching.

Herbert J. Cohen, M.D.

Herbert J. Cohen is currently the Director of the Rose F. Kennedy Center University Affiliated Program and the Children's Evaluation and Rehabilitation Center at Albert Einstein College of Medicine. He is Professor of Pediatrics and Rehabilitation Medicine at Albert Einstein College of Medicine.

Cohen has been involved with service, training, research, technical assistance and advocacy activities in the Bronx, New York City, New York State and nationally for the past 26 years.

He has served as a member and Vice-Chairman of the President's Committee on Mental Retardation, as President of the American Association of University Affiliated Programs, and as Chairman of both the Section on Child Development and the Committee on Children with Disabilities of the American Academy of Pediatrics.

He served for four years on an NIH Study Section and on numerous advisory groups to foundations, charitable organizations, child care programs and New York state agencies including the New York State Developmental Disability Planning Council and the State Interagency Coordinating Council for PL 99-457. Cohen is a Fellow of the American Association on Mental Retardation.